JOINERY BASICS

Sam Allen

Sterling Publishing Co., Inc.   New York

Basics Series

Band Saw Basics

Cabinetry Basics

Finishing Basics

Joinery Basics

Radial Arm Saw Basics

Router Basics

Scroll Saw Basics

Sharpening Basics

Table Saw Basics

Other Books by Sam Allen

Cabinetry Basics

Making Cabinets & Built-Ins

Making Kitchen Cabinet Accessories

Remodelling & Repairing Kitchen Cabinets

Wood Finisher's Handbook

Wood Joiner's Handbook

Library of Congress Cataloging-in-Publication Data

Allen, Sam.
   Joinery basics / Sam Allen.
       p.   cm.
   Includes index.
   ISBN 0-8069-7234-3
    1. Joinery—Amateurs' manuals. I. Title.
TH5663.A57 1992
694'.6—dc20
                                       91-41312
                                        CIP

10 9 8 7 6

Published in 1992 by Sterling Publishing Company, Inc.
387 Park Avenue South, New York, N.Y. 10016
© 1992 by Sam Allen
Distributed in Canada by Sterling Publishing
% Canadian Manda Group, P.O. Box 920, Station U
Toronto, Ontario, Canada M8Z 5P9
Distributed in Great Britain and Europe by Cassell PLC
Villiers House, 41/47 Strand, London WC2N 5JE, England
Distributed in Australia by Capricorn Link Ltd.
P.O. Box 665, Lane Cove, NSW 2066
Manufactured in the United States of America
All rights reserved

Sterling ISBN 0-8069-7234-3

Contents

INTRODUCTION

Whenever you build something using two or more pieces of wood, some form of joinery must be used. In the following pages, you will learn how to make the most commonly used joints. Practically anything can be built with these joints. The joiner's box shown in Illus. i-1 and described in Chapter 12 is an example of the type of project that can be built using the joints explored in this book. This box is inspired by the type of boxes used by 19th-century woodworkers to store their tools.

There are many ways to make each joint. Because this book is directed towards beginners, I have chosen some of the easiest and most reliable methods. For most of the joints, I have included one or two hand-tool methods and some power-tool techniques. I have tried to keep the number of tools to a minimum. Inexpensive tools are shown very often in the illustrations, because these are the types of tools most beginners will be using. Occasionally, I will examine a specialized tool that can be used to make a particular joint, but I also give directions for making the joint with more common tools.

This book is divided into twelve chapters. The first one presents a basic core of information. This information includes a clarification of the terminology used throughout the book, a description of the different types of joints, an overview of the power tools the beginner may find himself most often using, and gluing and clamping and safety techniques.

Chapter 2 deals with dowel joints. (See Illus. i-1.) Dowel joints are basically butt joints (a joint in which the edge of the end of one board butts against the other) that are reinforced with wood pegs called dowels. They are strong joints used in cabinets, bookcases, and to join the parts of a chair or table legs to the rails.

Spline joints are the subject of Chapter 3. (See

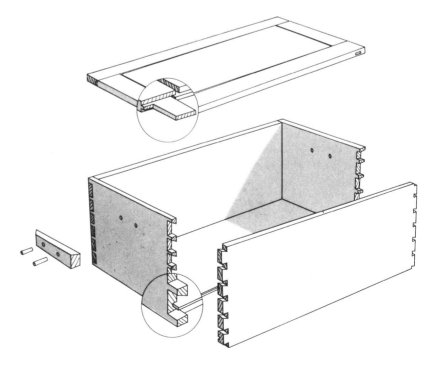

Illus. i-1. In the 19th century, a woodworker needed a strong box in which to store tools. The joinery of this box is typical of the type used in many antique reproductions—dovetails, mortise-and-tenon joints, tongue-and-groove joints, and pegged joints.

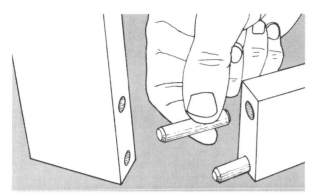

Illus. i-2. Dowel joint. (See Chapter 2.)

Illus. i-3. Spline joint. (See Chapter 3.)

Illus. i-3.) A spline joint is reinforced by a thin piece of wood called a spline. The spline fits into a groove that is cut into both mating surfaces of the joints. Spline joints are used in many of the same applications as dowel joints.

Chapter 4 covers rabbet joints. The rabbet joint is one of the most common joints used in cabinetmaking. (See Illus. i-4.) It is often used to join the top of a cabinet to its sides, and to attach the back of a cabinet.

Next comes a chapter on dado joints. Dado joints are used to make boxes, cabinets, and shelves. (See Illus. i-5.) Tongue-and-groove joints, the subject of Chapter 6, are two-part joints in which a projection on one board called a tongue fits into a groove in the other board. (See Illus. i-6.)

Lap joints are strong and easy to make. (See Illus. i-7.) They are used primarily to make frames, including cabinet and door frames. Lap joints are explored in Chapter 7.

Mitre joints are a highly decorative joint that is used extensively in finish carpentry or in any project where they will be highly visible, such as picture frames. (See Illus. i-8.) Refer to Chapter 8 for information on making mitre joints.

One of the strongest types of joints, the mortise-and-tenon joint, is explored in Chapter 9. In this joint, a projection called a tenon on one board fits into a pocket called a mortise in the other board. (See Illus. i-9.)

The box joint, the subject of Chapter 10, is a

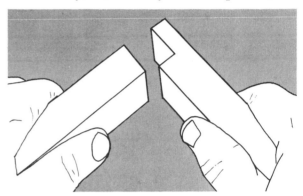

Illus. i-4. Rabbet joint. (See Chapter 4.)

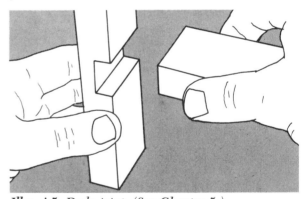

Illus. i-5. Dado joint. (See Chapter 5.)

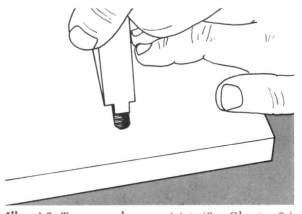

Illus. i-6. Tongue-and-groove joint. (See Chapter 6.)

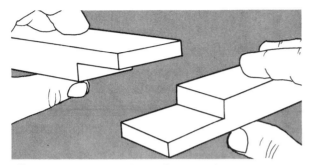

Illus. i-7. Lap joint. (See Chapter 7.)

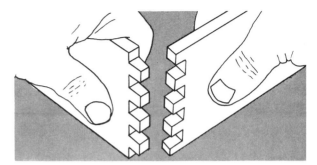

Illus. i-10. Box joint. (See Chapter 10.)

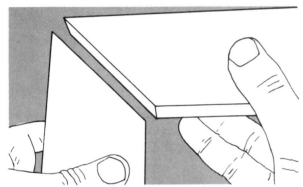

Illus. i-8. Mitre joint. (See Chapter 8.)

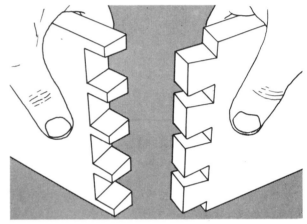

Illus. i-11. Dovetail joint. (See Chapter 11.)

Illus. i-9. Mortise-and-tenon joint. (See Chapter 9.)

strong joint usually used to make boxes. It has multiple interlocking fingers. (See Illus. i-10.)

The dovetail joint has always been considered a mark of fine craftsmanship. (See Illus. i-11.) It has wedge-shaped tails on one board that fit into the sockets on the other board. Chapter 11 explores dovetails.

The final chapter, Chapter 12, presents beginners with an opportunity to put the information they learned in the previous chapters to practical use. It contains directions for building the joiner's box shown in Illus. i-1. Even if you don't build the joiner's box, you can learn how several joints can be used to build a single project by following the project from beginning to end. Building the joiner's box is a useful exercise, because it will give you some practice with several important joints.

The text, photographs, and drawings presented in the following pages will clarify how to make and use an array of joints. In addition, pages 123 and 124 contain a glossary that defines both specific joint-making terms and general woodworking ones. Please refer to this glossary when you come across an unfamiliar term.

The joints explored in the following pages are the most commonly used and practical ones. There are many more joints that can be made, but they are used in specialized situations, and often one of the more common joints covered here can be used in the same applications. If you are interested in these more unusual joints, they are covered in my book *Wood Joiner's Handbook*.

Sam Allen

Chapter 1

JOINT-MAKING BASICS

Terminology

Wood joiners use a few specialized terms that you should know. These terms will be referred to in the directions that follow.

The first group of terms define or characterize a board. *Grain* refers to the orientation of the fibres in the wood. When the wood was part of a tree, the fibres were oriented with their length running up and down the tree's trunk. When wood is cut into boards, the grain runs with the length of the board. Grain is a term also used to describe the visible pattern of pores and growth rings.

Grain direction is an important factor in joinery. Wood breaks easily when stress is applied parallel to the grain. Wood does *not* break easily when stress is applied at a 90-degree angle to the grain.

If you aren't familiar with the way grain direction can affect the strength of a board, try this simple experiment: Cut two pieces of wood 2 inches wide and about 12 inches long. Cut the first one with the grain running with the length of the board, and the second one with the grain running across the board. Now, hold the ends of each of the boards and press the center of the board against the corner of the workbench. The board that has grain running with its length will be very hard to break, but the other board will snap easily in two. With this example in mind, think about the parts of different joints when you make them. If a small projection has the grain running the wrong way, it is likely to snap off under stress.

Each surface of a board has a name. (See Illus. 1-1.) A board has two *faces*. The faces are the two flat surfaces that are wider than the other surfaces of the board. The narrower flat surfaces that are parallel to the grain are called *edges*. The flat surfaces that are at a right angle to the grain are called *ends*.

Face grain refers to the direction of the wood fibres on the face of the board. The fibre orientation depends on the way the board was cut from the log. *Edge grain* is the term applied to the fibre orientation of the board edge. Since the ends are at a right angle to the grain, *end grain* refers to the porous ends of the fibres.

Terms that apply only to particular joints will be defined in the appropriate chapter, but there are some terms that apply to many different joints. A *through joint* is cut all the way through one board so that the end grain of the other board shows on the face of the first one. (See Illus. 1-2.)

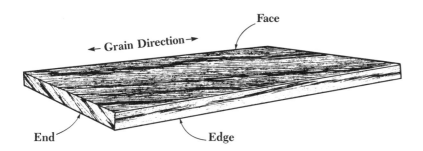

Illus. 1-1. To understand the instructions in this book, you need to be familiar with the basic terminology used. Shown here is a board and the terms used to define its basic parts.

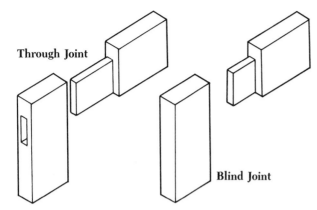

Illus. 1-2. *Through joints are cut all the way through the board, while blind joints only go part-way through. Shown here is a through mortise-and-tenon joint and a blind mortise-and-tenon joint.*

A *blind joint* is cut only partially through the board so that the end grain is hidden. No end grain shows on either face of a full blind joint. End grain is hidden on the front face of a *half-blind joint*, but shows on the other face.

When the part of the board that fits into a joint must be thinner or narrower than the rest of the board, the part of the joint that is cut 90 degrees to the face or edge of the board is called a *shoulder*. The part of the joint that is parallel with the face or edge is called a *cheek*. (See Illus. 1-3.) The standard versions of some joints require shoulder cuts. If a variation on that joint eliminates one or more of the shoulders, the joint is called a *bare-faced* joint.

Another important term that is used in this book is *kerf*. A kerf is the area that is cut away by a saw blade.

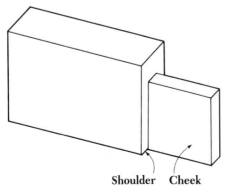

Illus. 1-3. *A tenon, and its shoulder and cheek.*

Types of Joint

The simplest joint is the butt joint. A butt joint is simply the edge or end of one board butted against another board. It is not very strong, and it almost always needs to be reinforced. Screws and nails are common ways to reinforce a butt joint. Dowels and splines can also be used to reinforce butt joints.

Four basic types of butt joint can be used to join boards together. All of the joints that appear in the following pages fall into one of these four general groups. (See Illus 1-4.) *Panel joints* are used to join two or more narrow boards together with a larger panel. *Edge joints* are used to join the edge of one board to the face of another. They are often used when applying trim or face frames to a cabinet. *Frame joints* join the end of one board to the edge of another board. They are used to make door frames and similar items.

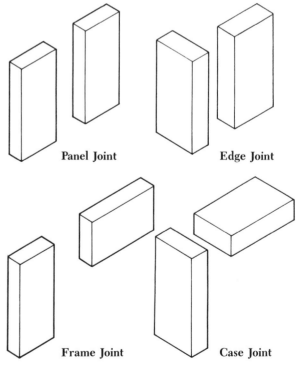

Illus. 1-4. *Four basic types of butt joints can be used to join boards together. They are the panel joint, the edge joint, the frame joint, and the case joint.*

Case joints join the end of one board to the face of another. They are used to make boxes, cabinets, and shelves. Case and frame joints can be L- or T-shaped. (See Illus. 1-5.)

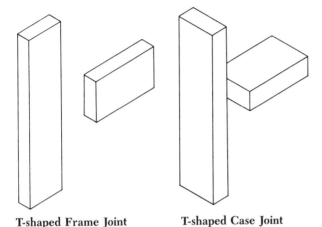

T-shaped Frame Joint   **T-shaped Case Joint**

Illus. 1-5. T-shaped frame and case joints.

Panel joints and edge joints are the strongest types of butt joint. This is because of the grain direction in the two joining parts. End grain doesn't glue well; it is too porous, so any joint on which end grain is glued will be weak. Most butt joints will have end grain on one of the boards. Panel and edge joints are two exceptions. On panel joints, edge grain is glued to edge grain. On edge joints, edge grain is glued to face grain. Both of these combinations result in a strong joint.

Gluing and Clamping Techniques

A good glue bond is essential to the strength of most joints. Using proper gluing and clamping techniques when assembling the joint will ensure a strong joint.

First, choose a quality glue. For most applications, aliphatic resin woodworking glue is a good choice. It is water-resistant. However, it won't stand up to wet exterior conditions, so use an exterior glue for those applications.

How you apply the glue is also important. Many woodworkers simply run a bead of glue along the joint and rely on the pressure of assembling the joint to spread the glue. This method tends to leave glue-starved areas in the joint. Instead, spread the glue around on both surfaces of the joint to achieve maximum strength. Begin by running a bead of glue on the joint; then spread it over the entire joint surface with your finger, a small brush, or a scrap of wood. The coat of glue should cover the wood completely, but make sure that it is not too thick. Coat the other surface of the joint in the same way.

It is important that you use enough glue. If not, the results will be a weak, glue-starved joint. However, try not to add too much glue; this will just cause a mess.

When the right amount of glue has been used, a small, uniform bead will be squeezed out of the joint as you clamp it. If no glue squeezes out, not enough glue was used. With some experience, you will be able to judge the proper amount of glue to use.

When a small amount of glue has been squeezed out, the best way to remove it is to let the glue set a while until it has begun to gel. Then use a chisel to scrape the glue from the board; wipe the glue from the chisel often so that it won't smear on the face of the board. If you used too much glue and it is dripping all over, you may need to use a rag to remove the excess glue. This will smear glue on the face of the board, making it difficult to stain. When there is a lot of excess glue, you may need to use a wet rag; be aware, however, that using a wet rag will dilute the glue, making it flow into the pores of the wood. Unless you remove all of the glue, the area will not stain well. The best method is to use the right amount of glue in the first place and avoid a messy cleanup.

Once the glue is spread on the joint, you have a limited amount of open time. Open time is the time you have to assemble the joint before the glue starts to set. It varies, depending on the type of glue being used. A long open time makes assembly easier, but it means that the glue will take longer to set. It is a good idea to apply glue only to one or two joints at a time when possible so that you can assemble the joint without rushing.

The joint must be held together tightly while the glue sets. Joints that are reinforced with screws or nails are held together by these reinforcements, but other joints must be clamped as the glue sets. There are many types of clamps. Three of the most common are the C-clamp, the handscrew clamp, and the bar clamp. The clamp you choose depends on the spread necessary. Handscrew clamps and C-clamps come in various sizes; the largest ones can usually handle a spread of about 10 inches.

When a larger spread is needed, use a bar clamp. Bar clamps can be adjusted to any size needed; the only limiting factor is the length of the bar. The least-expensive type of bar clamp has an ordinary steel-pipe bar; you buy the ends and any length of pipe needed. Pipe couplings can be used to increase the length of the bar if necessary. More expensive bar clamps use an I-beam bar.

When clamping a joint, place a scrap of wood between the jaws of the clamp and the work; this will prevent dents or marks on the work. Tighten the clamps until the joint pulls together and a small bead of glue squeezes out. Don't overtighten the clamps, because you may squeeze out too much glue, and the joint will be glue-starved.

Tools

All of the joints described in this book can be made with standard woodworking tools. In most cases instructions for making the joint with basic hand tools are given first, followed by instructions for using power tools. You need to be familiar with basic hand tools to follow the instructions in this book.

There are two power tools that are used extensively in joinery: the table saw and the router.

Almost every section includes directions for making the joint using one or both of these tools. If you are unfamiliar with the operation of these tools, refer to *Router Basics* or *Table Saw Basics*. Illus. 1-6 and 1-7 are drawings that clarify the different parts of these tools.

The table saw is a stationary power tool with a circular saw blade mounted below the table. (See Illus. 1-6.) The work can be guided with either the fence or mitre gauge. The fence is a guide that attaches to the table parallel to the blade. It is usually used to guide rip cuts (cuts made with the length of the board).

The mitre gauge is a moveable guide that fits in a slot in the table top. It can be adjusted to various angles. It is usually used to guide crosscuts (cuts made across the width of the board). The blade height adjustment controls how far the blade projects above the table. The blade tilt adjustment tilts the blade on an angle for making bevels and mitre cuts.

The table saw should be equipped with a blade guard. Use the guard whenever possible. Don't make freehand cuts on the table saw; always use either the fence or the mitre gauge to guide the work. Keep your fingers away from the blade. To keep your fingers safe, use a push stick to push the board.

The router is a portable power tool. (See Illus. 1-7.) It uses a small bit turning at high speeds to make a cut. Bits are available in many specialized shapes. For joinery, the three most useful ones are the straight bit, the rabbet bit, and the dovetail bit. The bit fits into a chuck or collet on the end of the motor shaft. The router base supports the router on the work. The depth-of-cut adjustment sets the distance that the bit projects below the router base.

Some routers are called plunge routers. They have a spring-loaded base. This is a very useful feature for joinery, because it enables you to make plunge cuts. A plunge cut begins or ends without breaking through to the edge of the board. A mortise is an example of a joint that can be cut with a plunge router. A plunge router has an adjustable depth stop. This controls the maximum depth of the bit.

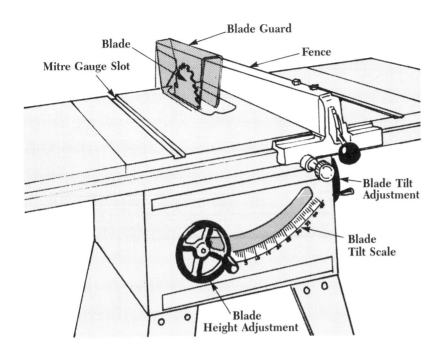

Illus. 1-6. *The controls and parts that are commonly found on table saws.*

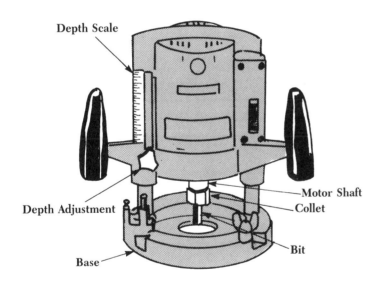

Illus. 1-7. *The controls and parts that are commonly found on routers.*

To make a plunge cut, begin with the bit raised completely above the base. Place the router in position and turn it on; then push down on the handles and lower the bit into the wood.

A router can be guided freehand or with fences and jigs. A router fence is an accessory that attaches to the base of the router. It will guide the router in a straight line parallel to the edge of the board. When the cut is too far from an edge to use the fence, or if it is at an angle to the edge, clamp a board to the work to guide the cut. The base of the router rubs against the board.

Specialized jigs can be purchased or made to guide a router. In this book, I describe how to make a dado and a mortise-and-tenon jig and how to use a commercial dovetail jig. Some jigs require the use of a template-following collar. This is a small collar or bushing that fits in the router base around the bit. The outside of the collar rubs against the edge of the jig template to guide the cut. Some bits incorporate a pilot. This is a small shaft or bearing on the end of the bit. The pilot will follow the edge of the board, making fences or jigs unnecessary.

Wear eye protection when you use a router, because small chips can fly out of the cut. Always clamp the work securely so that it won't slip as you are routing. Read and follow the manufacturer's instructions carefully before operating a router or any other power tool.

Safety Techniques

Woodworking can be an enjoyable activity if you are careful and follow all safety procedures, but if you get careless, serious accidents are possible. Be aware of safety at all times. Pay careful attention to all of the following guidelines:

1. Keep your tools sharp and maintain them properly. A dull tool is unsafe, because you must exert extra pressure to make it cut; as you do, you will be off balance and more likely to slip and get your hands or other parts of your body in the way of the cutting edge.

2. Clamp the work to a bench when possible so that you can use both hands to guide the tools.

3. Keep your hands away from the cutting edge of tools.

4. Wear the proper safety equipment when woodworking. Always wear safety glasses or goggles. When using a tool that throws a lot of chips, wear a full face shield in addition to your safety glasses. When using loud power equipment, wear hearing protectors. Wear a dust mask when sanding or doing other operations that produce a lot of dust.

5. Do not wear loose clothing and jewelry. They can get caught in the moving parts of power equipment and pull you into the machine. Long hair can also get caught in machinery, so tie it back when you operate power equipment.

6. Read the instructions that come with your tools and follow the manufacturer's safety and operating recommendations.

7. Use all safety equipment on the tools. Use the guards that come with your tools. (See Illus. 1-8.) In some photos in this book, the guards were removed to show the operation more clearly, but you should perform the operation with the guard in place. Use push sticks to keep your hands well away from the cutting edge of power equipment.

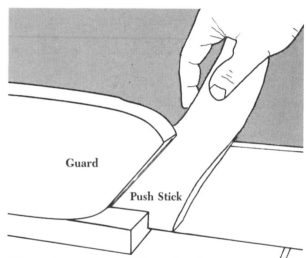

Illus. 1-8. Be sure to follow all safety precautions when woodworking. Use the guards that come with your tools, and keep your fingers away from the blade by using push sticks.

8. Never work when you are under the influence of drugs or alcohol. Even over-the-counter and perscription drugs can cause drowsiness or other effects that would make it dangerous to use tools, so read the labels and follow your doctor's advice.

9. Keep your mind on your work and avoid distractions. Think through each procedure before you do it. Don't do it if you feel it presents a safety hazard.

Chapter 2

DOWEL JOINTS

Dowel joints are easy to make, strong, and versatile. They are basically butt joints that are reinforced with wood pegs called dowels. They are used on many pieces of commercial furniture. Dowel joints can be used for panel, edge, frame, and case joints. When you can see the end of the dowel on one face of the joint, it is called a *pegged dowel joint.* When the dowels are completely hidden, the joint is called a *blind dowel joint.*

When to Use a Dowel Joint

Dowel joints can be used for practically any application. They are often used to join the stiles and rails of a cabinet face frame. (See Illus. 2-1.) They can also be used to join together the carcass of the cabinet. (The carcass is the basic frame of the cabinet.)

Many commercially made kitchen cabinets are made with dowel joints. Bookcases and other types of cabinets can also be made using dowel joints. Dowels can be used to join together the parts of a chair or to join table legs to the rails.

Equipment and Supplies

To make dowel joints, you will need dowels, a drill, drill bits, and, for some of the joints, a special dowel jig. These items are explored below.

Dowels

Dowels are made of hardwood and come in various sizes. The most useful dowels for general

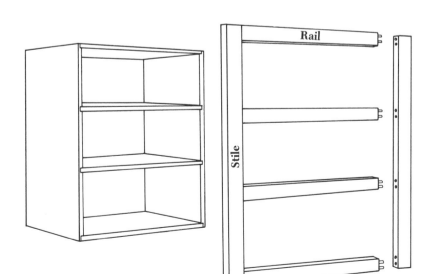

Illus. 2-1. Dowel joints can be used to join the stiles and rails of a cabinet face frame.

woodworking come in diameters of ¼, ⁵⁄₁₆, ⅜, and ½ inch. The diameter you use depends on the thickness of the wood being joined. For ¾-inch-thick boards, a ⁵⁄₁₆-inch dowel is a good choice. Generally, the dowel's diameter should be between one-third and one-half the thickness of the board.

You can buy dowel stock in three-foot lengths and cut your own dowel pins, or buy ready-made dowel pins. For most joinery uses, I use ready-made pins. They are cut to length and have chamfered ends. (See Illus. 2-2.) Ready-made dowel pins are available with either spiral grooves or straight fluting. The grooves or fluting allow excess glue and air to escape as the dowels are inserted into the holes. They also allow the glue to spread evenly throughout the joint.

Drills

A portable electric drill can be used for most dowelling operations. A drill press can be handy if you have one, but it is not necessary.

A good drill bit is a necessity. A brad-point bit is a good choice. It has a spur in the center that keeps the bit from wandering as you start the hole. Use a bit that is the same size as the dowels you will be using. Multi-flute dowels will be slightly oversize; if you use the same size drill bit as the standard size marked on the package, the dowel will be slightly larger to give a good, snug fit.

Jigs

A dowel jig helps to position the hole and keeps the bit straight as you drill. There are many types of dowel jig on the market. They don't all function the same way or make the same type of joints, so you should decide what types of dowel joints you will be making before you buy a jig. Two types of jigs are depicted in the illustrations in this chapter. The first one is a Stanley #59. (See Illus. 2-3.) It is representative of a number of jigs that can be used to make frame and panel joints. The Stanley jig clamps to the edge or end of a board. Several sizes of interchangeable bushings are used to guide the drill bit. To center the hole position, you loosen a wing nut and align a mark with a graduated scale. Another similar jig is the General #840. This jig operates about the same as the Stanley, but a rotating turret is used instead of the loose bushings.

Some jigs are self-centering, which means that the holes will be drilled close to the center of the board no matter what the thickness of the board. The holes will not be drilled exactly in the center of the board, so to ensure a perfect fit always

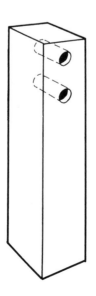

Illus. 2-2. Commercially made dowel pins have chamfered ends that make them easier to insert. They also have grooves that allow air and glue to escape from the hole as the dowel is inserted. Drill the dowel holes about ¹⁄₁₆ inch deeper than the length of the dowel, to allow room for excess glue.

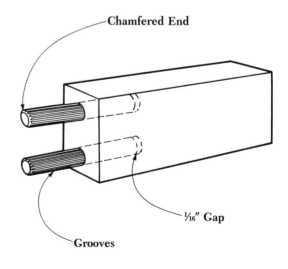

Chamfered End

¹⁄₁₆″ Gap

Grooves

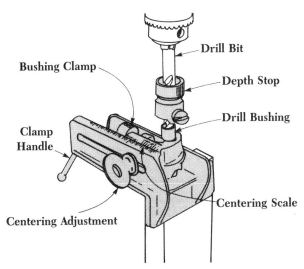

Illus. 2-3. Stanley #59 dowelling jig.

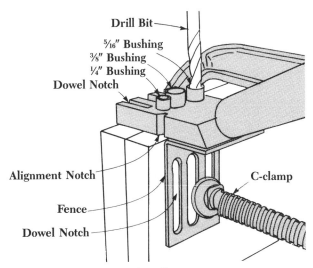

Illus. 2-4. Arco #582 dowelling jig.

position the jig so that the fence is against the same face on both boards. This will compensate for any error. The Dowel-it 1000 is an example of a self-centering jig.

To make case and edge joints, you will need a different type of jig. In the appropriate illustrations that follow, the Arco #582 jig is shown. (See Illus. 2-4.) This jig can be used to make case, edge, frame, and panel joints. It doesn't have a built-in clamp, so you must use a C-clamp to hold it in place. It has three built-in bushings for ¼-, 5/16-, and ⅜-inch bits. There is no provision for centering the holes. The bushings are prepositioned so that the ¼-inch hole is approximately centered on a ½-inch-thick board, the 5/16-inch hole will be close to the center of a ¾-inch-thick board, and the ⅜-inch hole is near the center of a 1-inch-thick board. This lack of adjustment is the one limitation of this jig, but it is not usually a problem if you are careful to always place the jig fence against the same face on both boards.

This type of jig has notches that allow you to align the jig for the second set of holes by placing the notch over a dowel placed in the previously drilled holes in the mating board. This simplifies the joint layout.

Two other jigs that can be used for case and edge joints are the Disston Dowel Magic and the Wolfcraft Dowel-Master. The Disston jig is self-centering, but it only has one size of bushing, so you need a separate jig to drill another size of hole. The Wolfcraft jig has bushings for ¼-, 5/16- and ⅜-inch drill bits.

There are several other dowel jigs on the market. Most of them operate about the same way as the ones just described. Before buying one, make sure that it is capable of making the type of joints needed.

Making Dowel Joints

Pegged Joints

As mentioned earlier, the end of the dowel on one face of a pegged joint is *not* hidden. Pegged joints are the easiest dowel joints to make. The joint is assembled first, and then the holes are drilled. A jig is not needed to make a pegged joint, and the exposed ends of the dowels add a decorative touch that can make the project more interesting looking. Pegged joints can be used in edge, case, and some frame joints, but not in panel joints. (See Illus. 2-5.)

The key to making any dowel joint is to first make a butt joint that fits together well. Cut the ends of the boards square and straight. Lay out the peg locations. Use at least two or three pegs per joint, more if the joint is long. The pegs should be about 1 inch in from the edges, to

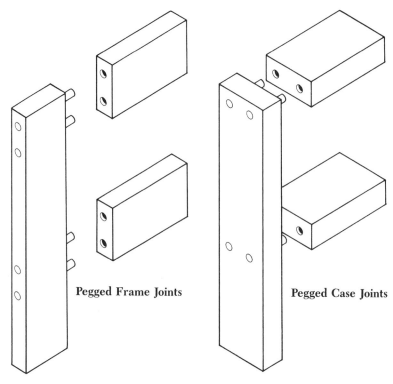

Illus. 2-5. Pegged joints can be used in every application except panel joints. In a pegged joint, the dowel extends all the way through one board and into the mating board. Use a dowel of contrasting color for decorative effect.

Pegged Frame Joints

Pegged Case Joints

prevent the board from splitting. Now, assemble the joint. Apply glue to the joint surfaces and clamp the joint together.

Next, drill the holes. Place a piece of tape on the bit to indicate how deep to drill the holes. The hole depth should be about twice the thickness of the board. Angle the drill slightly towards the center of the board when you drill the two outside holes. This will improve the strength of the joint, making it harder to pull apart. (See Illus. 2-6.)

Put glue about one-third of the way into the holes. Then use a piece of scrap wood to spread the glue around inside the hole. Drive dowel pins into the holes. The pins should be a little longer than necessary.

Use a fine-tooth saw to trim the dowels close to the surface of the board. Trim close to the surface, but leave enough space between the saw and the board so that you don't chew up the surface of the board as you cut. Sand the dowels flush. Either sand them by hand with sandpaper wrapped around a block of wood or use a power belt sander to do the job quickly.

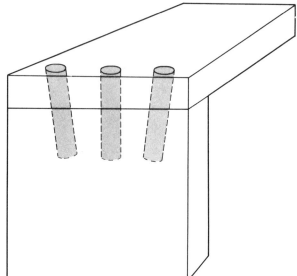

Illus. 2-6. Angling the dowels in a pegged joint locks the joint together. You can't angle the dowels in a blind joint, so the pegged joint is the better joint to use when you need maximum strength.

Blind Dowel Joints

The dowels in a blind dowel joint are completely concealed. This joint is often used when clean, modern-looking lines are desired. Blind dowel joints can be used for panel, edge, frame, and case joints. (See Illus. 2-7.)

Blind joints are usually made with a dowelling jig. The jig aligns the holes and guides the drill bit. Dowel centers, a marking tool, can be used instead of a jig to align the holes for a blind dowel joint. (See pages 24 and 25.) You can make blind dowel joints without a jig or dowel centers by using careful layout procedures.

Panel Joints

When a wide board is needed, you can glue several narrow boards together into a panel. Panel joints are very strong even without any reinforcement. This is because edge grain is being glued to edge grain, which forms a very strong gluing bond. So, if you prefer, simply leave out the dowels and follow these directions to make a panel butt joint. However, one disadvantage of a

panel butt joint is that the boards tend to slip out of alignment as they are being clamped. A few dowels in the joint will keep the boards aligned as you assemble them. Since you aren't relying on the dowels for strength, you don't need a lot of them. One dowel per foot is sufficient. If there is a particular problem area where a board has a bow in it that has to be pulled out, then add more dowels.

Cut the board to rough length a little longer than necessary. Make a trial layout of the panel. The grain direction is important in panel layout, because any tendency for cupping will be exaggerated if the boards are not placed properly. Look at the end grain. You will be able to see the growth rings. These are the semi-circular grain patterns. Place the boards so that the direction of the growth rings alternates from one board to the next.

When you have positioned all of the boards, draw a large V across the boards. This will help

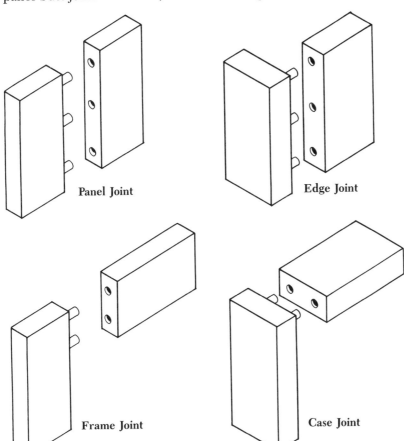

Panel Joint

Edge Joint

Frame Joint

Case Joint

Illus. **2-7.** *Blind dowel joints can be used with all four types of joints. The dowel holes don't go all the way through the board, so there is no visible evidence of the joint.*

you to reposition the boards as you glue up the panel, and to determine which boards mate together as you drill the dowel joints. In the directions that follow, the term *marked face* refers to the face of the board that has the pencil V marks.

The most important factor in making a strong panel joint is getting the two edges to fit together well. The edges should be smooth, square (at right angles to each other), and true. If you are using dimensional lumber, the edges have been jointed (smoothed, squared, and trued) at the mill. If the edge is still true (not curved), then you can use the factory edges. This is probably the easiest method for the beginner. Sight down the edge of the board to determine if it is true.

You can rip a board into narrower boards using the table saw. If you start with a true edge to ride against the rip fence, then the cut edge will usually be straight and true enough to use without further jointing.

When you are using boards that don't have a true edge, you will have to joint them. A jointer is a power tool that can be used to produce a smooth, square, and true edge. Set the fence to 90 degrees. Set the depth of cut to about ⅙ inch. Hold the board with the edge against the table and the face against the fence. Keep your hands well away from the cutting head and keep all guards in place. Run the board through at a steady, moderate pace. Refer to the directions that come with the jointer for complete instructions.

Boards can be jointed by hand with a plane. Shooting boards are useful accessories that will make it easier for a beginner to get a good edge. Simple shooting boards can be made from two pieces of ¾-inch-thick board. The size of the shooting board depends on the size of board being planed; you can make it as long or wide as needed. However, the shooting boards should be slightly longer than the boards being planed. Make sure that the shooting boards have edges that are straight.

Place the board to be planed between the two shooting boards, in a vise. The shooting boards should be positioned so they are slightly lower than the lowest point on the edges to be planed.

Align the top edges of the shooting boards with a square.

Set the plane to make a shallow cut. Now, hold the plane on an angle so that the area in front of its cutting edge will ride on one shooting board and the area behind the cutting edge will ride on the other shooting board. (See Illus. 2-8.) Begin by planing the spots that project above the shooting board more than the rest of the board. When these high spots are gone, make a few passes along the entire length of the boards to trim the board's edge so that it is level with the shooting boards.

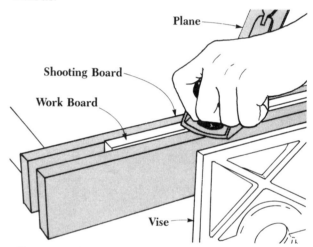

Illus. 2-8. The secret to a successful dowel joint is to make the mating surfaces straight and square. You can use shooting boards and a hand plane to true-up the edge of a board. The shooting boards help you guide the plane. Stop planing as soon as the plane touches the shooting boards.

When all of the edges have been jointed, lay out the dowel positions. Place two mating boards together with the mating edges up and the marked faces out. (See Illus. 2-9.) Align the ends of the boards and temporarily clamp them together. The first dowel should be located about two inches in from the end of the board. Use a square to draw a line across both boards. The rest of the dowels should be about one foot apart until you get to approximately two inches from the end of the board; here, mark the final dowel location.

Now, set up the dowelling jig. Adjust it to center the hole on the edge of the board, and then

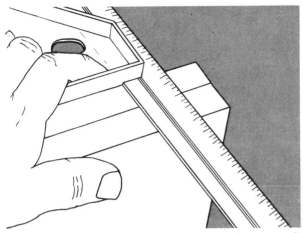

Illus. 2-9. To lay out the dowel locations for a panel joint, place the boards with their inside faces together. Line up their ends, and place a clamp on the boards to hold the alignment. Use a square to draw a line across the edge of both boards at each dowel location.

Illus. 2-10. This type of dowelling jig works well for panel joints. Place it on the edge of the board and align the index mark on the jig with the layout mark on the board. Tighten the clamp, and then drill the hole. The depth stop on the bit can be set to determine the depth of the hole.

insert the correct bushing. For most panel joints, you can use ¼-inch dowels, so insert the ¼-inch bushing into the jig. Place the dowel jig over the first dowel location. The fence should be placed against the marked face of the board. Align the index mark on the jig with the position line on the edge of the board. Clamp the jig in place.

Put the drill bit in the drill chuck and position the depth stop on the bit. Instead of a commercial depth stop, wrap a piece of tape around the drill bit to indicate the depth of the hole. The hole should be about ¹⁄₁₆ inch deeper than half the length of the dowel pin. Put the drill bit into the dowel jig and drill down until the tape touches the top of the jig. (See Illus. 2-10.)

Remove the jig and move to the next location. When all of the holes have been drilled in one board, start on the mating board. Make sure that you keep the fence of the jig on the marked face of the board. This will compensate for any errors in the centering of the jig.

When a panel is made from more than two boards, glue and assemble each joint individually. If you try to glue and assemble the joints all at once, the glue may set before you have a chance to get the clamps on. Spread an even coat of glue on both mating surfaces. Since the dowels

in this joint are used more for alignment than reinforcement purposes, simply let a little glue drip into the dowel holes. It does not have to be spread evenly around in the hole. Insert the dowels into the holes in one board and drive them in with a hammer.

Put the boards edge to edge and align the dowels on the one board with the holes in the other board. If one of the boards is bowed, press down on it as you align the dowels. Use bar clamps to draw the boards together. Place scrap boards between the clamp jaws and the edges of the boards to prevent the clamp from denting the edges. Alternate the clamps so that one is on top and the next one underneath. This will equalize the clamping pressure and keep the panel flat.

If you are just gluing together two boards, simply leave the clamps on for about one hour as the glue sets, and then remove them. If you are gluing together more than two boards, remove the clamps as soon as you put the boards together, and apply glue to the next set of edges. Insert the dowels and clamp the next board to the panel. When the final board is in place, leave the clamps on until the glue sets.

Frame Joints

Frame joints are used to make face frames for cabinets and cabinet doors, and for joints between the stretchers and legs of chairs. This joint has one surface that is end grain. Glue won't hold this joint together without reinforcement, so the dowels are very important to the strength of the joint.

It is important that the end of the board be cut square. If it is out of square, the joint will be weak and the frame will be out of square, or there will be a visible gap in the joint. If you use a power saw such as a table saw or radial arm saw, make sure that it is adjusted to make a cut that is exactly 90 degrees. To cut the boards by hand, use a backsaw and a mitre box.

After the boards are cut, lay out the dowel locations. For boards up to 3 inches wide, use two dowels located ½ inch in from the edges. For wider boards, add a third dowel in the center. Place the two boards together the way they will be when assembled. Make a mark on the front face of each board, and number the joints. Now, reposition the boards so that they are side by side with their marked faces out. (See Illus. 2-11.) Clamp the boards together, and use a square to mark the dowel locations on both boards.

Now, set up the dowelling jig. Install the correct bushing for the size hole you need. For ½-

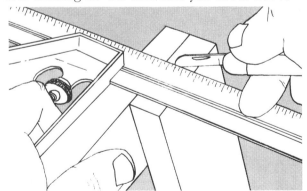

Illus. 2-11. To lay out a frame blind dowel joint, place the parts with their inside faces together. The end of one board should be flush with the edge of the other board. Clamp the boards together, and then use a square to mark a layout line across the end of the first board and the edge of the second at each dowel location.

inch-thick boards, use a ¼-inch hole. Boards ¾ inch thick need a ⁵⁄₁₆-inch hole, and 1-inch-thick boards require a ⅜-inch hole. Place the dowelling jig on the end of the first board with the fence against the marked face. Adjust the jig to center the hole. Align the index mark on the jig with the first layout mark, and clamp the jig in place.

Insert the drill bit in the drill chuck and set the depth stop on the bit. Drill the hole ¹⁄₁₆ inch deeper than one-half the length of the dowel. Drill the first hole, and then move on to the next one. (See Illus. 2-12.) When the first board is done, place the jig on the edge of the second board and drill the holes. Make sure that the jig fence is against the marked face.

Illus. 2-12. Clamp the dowelling jig to the end of the board to drill the dowel holes for a frame joint. The holes in the mating board are drilled into its edge.

The joint is now ready to assemble. Apply glue to the surface of the joint and spread it around to evenly coat both glue surfaces. A lot of the strength of the joint depends on a good glue bond between the dowels and the sides of the holes, so careful gluing technique is necessary. Fill the holes about one-third full of glue. Then use a splinter of wood to spread the glue inside the hole. Make sure that the sides of the hole are covered with an even coat of glue from top to bottom, and that there is not much glue left in the bottom of the hole. Insert the dowels into one of the boards, and drive them into the boards with a hammer.

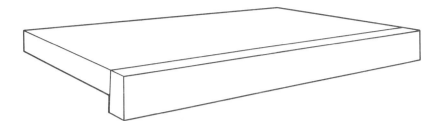

Illus. 2-13. Blind dowels can be used to attach edging to plywood or particleboard. This is often done when making shelves. The edging strip is usually 1½ inches wide.

Align the dowels on the one board with the holes in the other board and pull the joint tight with clamps. Leave the clamps in place until the glue sets.

Edge Joints

Edge joints are usually used to add edging to a shelf or in similar applications. When used with solid lumber, this joint joins edge grain to face grain. This also results in a strong glue bond. Glue alone will give this joint all the strength it needs, but dowels can be added to make alignment during assembly easier.

This joint is often used to add edging to hide the raw edges of plywood or particleboard. (Particleboard is a sheet material made from wood chips or wood particles.) (See Illus. 2-13.) These edges glue like end grain, so in this situation the dowels are necessary for added strength.

Like the panel joint, the edge joint requires a square and true edge. Use the shooting boards or a jointer to joint the edge if necessary. The factory-cut edges of plywood and particle board are usually very true. If you use the table saw to make the cuts and have a true edge to ride against the rip fence, jointing may not be necessary.

Lay out the dowel locations. Put the boards together in the position they will be assembled. Make a mark on the top face of the shelf and the top edge of the edging board. Now, remove the edging board and lay out the hole locations on the front edge of the shelf. Locate the outside dowels about two inches in from the ends, and then space the remaining dowels about one foot apart.

Drill the holes in the edge of the shelf first. Place the dowel jig fence against the marked face. Use tape on the drill bit to gauge the depth

of each hole, or use a commercial depth stop that clamps onto the bit. The dowel will be inserted deeper into the shelf than into the edging. Set the depth stop to make a hole that is about ½ inch less than the total length of the dowel.

The jig has a feature that aligns the holes in the second board with the previously drilled holes. To use this feature, clamp the boards together in their proper orientation. Place the outside face of the edging board against the top face of the shelf. The top edge of the edging board should be flush with the front edge of the shelf. Insert dowels temporarily into the holes. Place the jig fence

Illus. 2-14. This type of jig can be used to make edge joints. Drill the holes in the shelf first. Then clamp the edging strip to the shelf, as shown here. Insert dowels into the holes in the shelf. Place the notch in the dowelling jig fence over one of the dowels, and clamp the jig in place. Set the depth stop to make a hole about ½ inch deep, and drill the holes.

against the top edge of the board and slip the aligning notch over the first dowel. Clamp the jig in place. Reset the depth stop to make a ½-inch-deep hole. Place the bit in the jig and drill the hole. (See Illus. 2-14.)

When all of the holes are drilled, spread a coat of glue evenly along both mating surfaces of the joint. Drip some glue into the dowel holes and insert a dowel into each hole in one of the boards. Align the dowels with the holes in the mating board, and assemble the joint. Clamp the joint and let the glue set.

Case Joints

Case joints are primarily used for building cabinets. The 32-millimetre system of cabinetmaking is a method of making cabinets without face frames. The face frame adds strength to traditional cabinets. To compensate for the lack of a face frame, a very strong joint is needed. The case blind dowel joint is used extensively in frameless 32-mm cabinets because of its strength and adaptability to mass production.

Case dowel joints can be used to make all kinds of cabinets from small bookshelves to a large hutch. (See Illus. 2-15.) There are two types of case joint. The L-shaped case joint is used at a corner. The T-shaped case joint is used in places such as a shelf or cabinet bottom. If you want complete directions for making cabinets using this joint, refer to my book *Cabinetry Basics*.

Not all dowel jigs can be used to make case joints, so be sure to get the right kind if you plan on making cabinets using dowel joints.

Begin making a blind case dowel joint by cutting the parts to size. A straight, square edge is essential to a good joint. Use a table saw, a radial arm saw, or a portable circular saw to cut the parts. If you use the portable saw, clamp a guide board to the work to guide the saw; this will ensure a straight edge. The guide board is a piece of plywood or particleboard with a straight factory edge. The edge of the saw base rubs against the guide board.

Next, lay out the dowel locations. For cabinet work, the industry standard is 32-mm spacing. Dowels are placed at multiples of 32 mm. In most cases, it is not necessary to place a dowel every 32 mm. Usually, you can use four dowels per joint.

Place the outside dowels in from the end

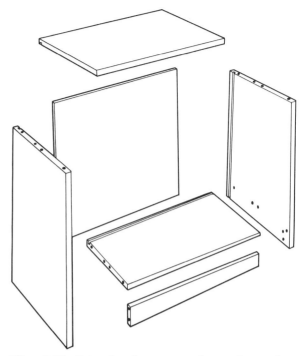

Illus. 2-15. Case dowel joints can be used to make cabinet carcasses. This exploded view of a cabinet shows how the dowels are arranged.

16 mm. Then find the center of the board and measure 16 mm on either side of the center line. This will give you two dowel locations at the center that are spaced 32 mm apart. For added strength, add additional dowels spaced 64 mm apart.

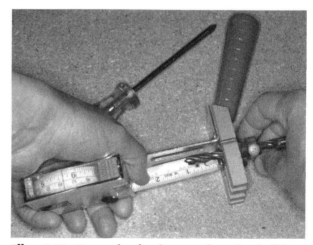

Illus. 2-16. To set the depth stop, place the drill bit in the bushing on the dowelling jig. Measure from the bottom of the jig to the tip of the drill bit, and then tighten the depth stop.

Set the depth stop on the drill bit. Insert the bit into the jig and measure from the bottom of the jig to the tip of the bit. (See Illus. 2-16.) Position the dowel jig over the first hole location and clamp it in place. Drill the hole; then reposition the dowelling jig and drill the rest of the holes. (See Illus. 2-17.)

Illus. 2-17. Drill the holes into the end of the board. Clamp large boards to the side of a sawhorse. Place the dowelling jig over the first hole location and clamp it in place. Drill the hole; then move to the next dowel location.

The dowelling jig has a feature that allows you to use the holes in the first board to guide the jig when drilling the holes in the mating board. Place dowels in the holes temporarily while you drill the next set of holes. For an L-shaped joint, clamp the two boards with their outside faces together. Place the jig on the work with the positioning notch in the fence over the dowel in the other board. Clamp the jig in place. (See Illus. 2-18.)

For T-shaped joints, remove the fence from the jig. Draw a line on the board to indicate the location of the bottom of the mating board. Put dowels temporarily into the holes in the mating board. Place the mating board on top of the other board, with the inside faces of the boards together. Align the edges of the boards. Place the jig on top of the bottom board. Butt the end of the jig against the end of the top board. Move the jig and top board until the positioning notch on

Illus. 2-18. To drill the mating holes in an L-shaped joint, place the parts with their outside faces together. Align the ends and edges, and then clamp them. Place the notch in the dowelling jig fence over a dowel that has been inserted into the previously drilled holes. Use a C-clamp to hold the jig in place.

Illus. 2-19. To drill the mating holes in a T-shaped joint, draw a layout line that indicates the location of the outside face of the board. Insert dowels into the holes already drilled in the end of the board. Place the boards with their inside faces together. Remove the fence from the dowelling jig. Butt the end of the jig against the end of the board that has the dowels. Slide the board and jig back and forth until the notch in the side of the jig lines up with the layout line, as shown here. Make sure that the edges of the boards are aligned correctly, and then clamp them together.

the side of the jig lines up with the layout line. (See Illus. 2-19.) Then clamp the boards together.

Place the notch in the jig over the first dowel and clamp it in place. Reset the depth stop on the drill bit. Make the hole in this board as deep as possible without drilling through the face. Drill the holes, repositioning the jig for each dowel location. (See Illus. 2-20.)

Illus. 2-20. Clamp the dowelling jig in place with a C-clamp, and drill the holes.

When you are making several joints that are alike, there is no need to lay out each joint. Once you have drilled the first set of holes, insert dowels in them and use the first joint as a guide for the dowelling jig for the rest of the joints.

Illus. 2-21. The first joint can be used to guide the dowelling jig for making the rest of the joints. This saves layout time. Clamp the boards together as shown here, and insert dowels into the holes in the first board. Place the notch in the dowelling jig over a dowel and clamp it in place; then drill the hole.

Clamp the parts together with the outside face of the first board against the inside face of the board to be drilled. Place the dowelling jig on the end of the boards, with the notch over a dowel and the fence against the outside face of the board to be drilled. (See Illus. 2-21.) After you have drilled the holes in the new board, insert dowels in the holes and use it to guide the jig as you drill the holes in the mating board.

To begin assembly, apply glue to the joint surfaces. Spread it evenly. Drip glue into the dowel holes and spread it in the hole using a splinter of wood. Place the dowels in the holes and drive them in with a hammer. (See Illus. 2-22.) Align

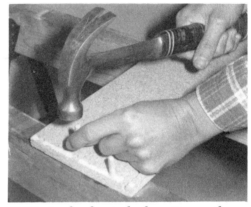

Illus. 2-22. Apply glue to both mating surfaces of the joint and spread glue inside the dowel holes. Drive the dowels into the holes in the first board with a hammer.

the dowels with the holes in the other board, and push them together. Use a hammer to drive the joint tight. Place a block of wood on top of the board and hit the block with the hammer to keep from denting the face of the board. (See Illus. 2-23.) Pull the joint tight with clamps. Leave the clamps in place until the glue sets.

Dowel Centers

You can make blind dowel joints without a dowelling jig. Dowel centers can be used to transfer the location of holes in one board to the mating board. Dowel centers are metal plugs that fit into a dowel hole. They have sharp spurs in the exact

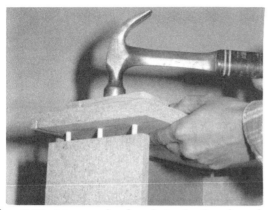

Illus. 2-23. Line up the dowels in the first board with the holes in the mating board. Drive the joint tight with a hammer. Use a block of wood to protect the face of the board from dents.

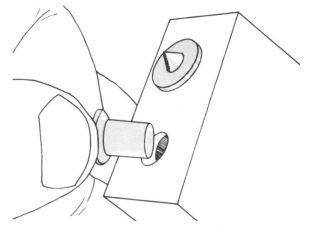

Illus. 2-24. Dowel centers can be used to transfer the location of the holes from one board to the mating board. A dowel center is a metal plug that fits in a dowel hole. It has a sharp spur in its center. First, drill the dowel holes into one board, and then insert the dowel centers.

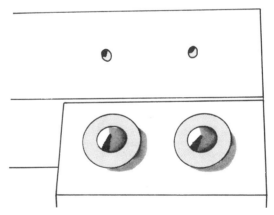

Illus. 2-25. Hold the boards in their proper alignment and press them together. The spurs will leave small dents in the mating board indicating the location of the hole.

center of the plug. The spur is used to make a mark on the mating board. Dowel centers can be used to make frame, panel, edge, and case joints. Both L- and T-shaped joints can be marked using dowel centers.

Begin by laying out the hole locations on the end of one of the boards. Next, drill holes at the marked locations. It is important that the holes be straight. A drill press can be used, but it is possible to guide a hand drill accurately enough. Put the work in a vise and hold the drill at arm's length so that you can sight along the drill bit. Adjust the way you hold the drill until the bit looks like it is at a 90-degree angle to the end of the board. Insert the dowel centers into the holes. (See Illus. 2-24.)

If you are making a frame joint, lay the mating board down on a flat surface and line up the joint. Push the joint together. The spurs on the dowel centers should make small marks in the mating board. (See Illus. 2-25.) If you are using a very hard wood, it may be necessary to tap the joint with a mallet to get the spurs to make a mark.

Panel joints are also marked with the faces of the boards placed on a flat surface. Case and edge joints are marked by placing the board to be marked inside, face-up, on a flat surface. Place the end of the board with the dowel centers on top of the other board, and line up the joint. Press down on the board to make the marks.

When making T-shaped joints, it can be helpful to clamp a guide board along the layout line on the board to be marked. Then place the board with the dowel centers against the guide board, and line up the edges.

Now, drill dowel holes into the second board. Place the spur of the brad-point drill bit on the mark left by the dowel center. Hold the drill bit square with the edge of the board. Once the holes are drilled, the assembly procedures are the same as described above.

Chapter 3

SPLINE JOINTS

Spline joints are reinforced by a thin piece of wood called a spline. The spline fits into a groove that is cut into both mating surfaces of the joint. Splines make the joint strong and easy to align during assembly. They can be used in panel, edge, frame, and case joints. (See Illus. 3-1.)

Spline grooves can be cut all the way across the board or made blind when it is desirable to hide the spline ends.

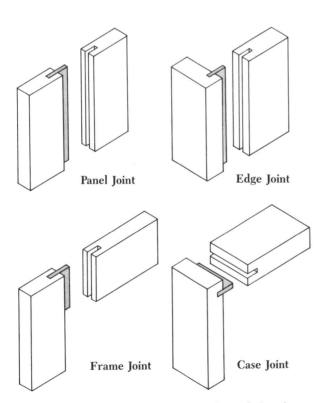

Panel Joint   **Edge Joint**

Frame Joint   **Case Joint**

Illus. 3-1. A spline is a thin strip of wood that fits into a groove. Splines can be used to reinforce many types of joints.

When to Use a Spline Joint

Spline joints are used in many of the same applications as dowel joints. Since the spline doesn't penetrate as deeply into the wood, frame joints made with splines are not as strong as dowel joints. In most other applications, splines are as strong or stronger than a dowel joint. Some common uses for spline joints include glued-up panels, panel door frames, small shelves, and contemporary furniture.

Making Spline Joints

Spline joints are usually made with power tools. Though the grooves can be cut with hand tools, it is much easier to use a router or table saw.

Splines

Splines can be made from hardwood, plywood, or hardboard. Hardboard is an ideal spline material for most applications. It has no grain direction, is strong, and is easy to work with. Most splines are made from ⅛-inch- or ¼-inch-thick material. Generally, the spline should be as wide as the thickness of the board. The spline should be no thicker than about one-third the thickness of the boards.

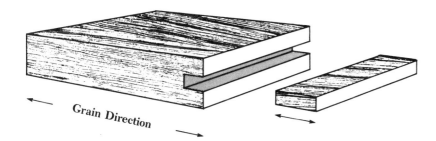

Grain Direction

Illus. 3-2. When making a case joint in solid lumber, orient the grain in the spline in the same direction as the grain in the boards.

Splines can be used with lumber, plywood, and particleboard. When used with plywood and particleboard, hardboard splines can be used in all applications. When you are using solid lumber, grain direction can be a factor. Solid lumber will shrink and swell across its width as the air humidity changes from season to season. If you use a hardboard spline in a case joint, the spline won't shrink and swell at the same rate as the boards. This can lead to joint failure or cracked boards. For case joints in solid lumber, use hardwood for the splines. The grain of the spline must be oriented the same way as the grain in the boards. This seems unusual at first, because usually the grain runs along the length of the board. In this instance, however, the grain must run across the width of the spline. (See Illus. 3-2.)

Hardboard splines can be used on panel and edge joints in solid lumber, because lumber doesn't change much in length with changes in humidity. Hardboard splines can also be used in frame joints.

Using a Table Saw

The table saw is an efficient tool for cutting spline grooves. If you are using ⅛-inch-thick material, you don't even need a special blade to make the groove. Most table saw blades leave a ⅛-inch-wide kerf. Simply lower the blade to one-half the board thickness. Then set the fence to center the spline groove. (See Illus. 3-3.)

To make a groove for a ¼-inch-thick spline, make two passes with the standard blade. Reposition the fence for the second pass so that the two kerfs are side by side.

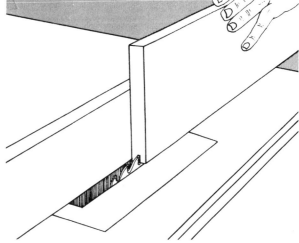

Illus. 3-3. A table saw can be used to make spline grooves. Set the fence to guide the cut. A piece of wood attached to the fence will help support wide boards.

A dado blade will make the groove in a single pass. Set the blade to make a ¼-inch groove. Position the fence to center the groove on the board.

Splined Panel Joint

The table saw can be used to make a splined panel joint. A panel joint is an edge-grain-to-edge-grain joint. Edge grain glues well, so reinforcement is not necessary. A simple butt joint is strong enough, but adding a spline makes it easier to align the boards during assembly and keeps them from slipping out of alignment as the clamps are tightened. If one of the boards is bowed, a spline will help you hold it flat as you clamp the joint.

Through Splined Joint In a through splined joint, the end of the spline will be visible. To make a through splined panel joint, begin by laying out the panel. Place the boards in their proper position, with their end-grain patterns alternated, and make a V mark on one face. Joint the edges of both boards as described in Chapter 2 for dowel-reinforced panel joints.

Since the spline in a panel joint is used mostly for alignment purposes, it only needs to be ⅛ inch thick. A standard table-saw blade can be used to make the groove. Raise the blade until it is ⅜ inch above the table. Set the fence to center the groove on the edge of the board. Place the board on the saw with its edge on the table and its marked face against the fence.

When making grooves on a large board, it will be helpful to add a wide extension to the fence, for additional support. This fence extension can be made from plywood or particleboard. The fence contains screw holes. Drive screws through these holes to secure the extension to the fence.

Turn on the saw and feed the board through the blade. (See Illus. 3-4.) Keep your fingers away from the blade. Use push sticks when necessary. Make the groove in the second board following the same procedure. By keeping the marked face of both boards against the fence, you will ensure that the joint will line up, even if the groove is off-center slightly.

Cut a ¾-inch-wide spline from ⅛-inch-thick hardboard. Sand the edges of the spline to remove the fuzz left by the saw. Apply an even coat of glue to both joint surfaces. Since the spline is mostly for alignment purposes, it is not important that you apply an even coat of glue in the groove. The glue that normally drips into the groove is all that is needed.

Insert the spline into one of the grooves. Assemble the joint, aligning the spline with the second groove. (See Illus. 3-5.) If one of the boards is bowed, you may need to press down on it while assembling the joint. It sometimes helps to start the spline in the groove at one end, and then work your way along the joint. Clamp the joint until the glue sets.

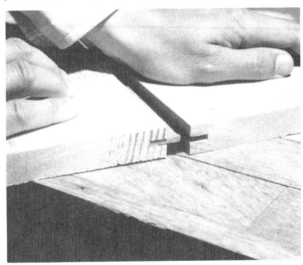

Illus. 3-5. Assembling a splined panel joint.

Blind Spline Joint   A blind joint requires more steps than a through joint. Use caution when making blind spline grooves, because there is a possibility of kickback. (Kickback occurs when a piece of stock is flung back at the operator at great speed.) Keep your fingers well away from the blade while working.

Begin by placing masking tape on the fence near the front and back of the blade. Next, make a mark on the tape at the exact location where the blade enters and exits the throat of the table insert. Make a mark on the face or edge of the board to indicate where you want the spline

Illus. 3-4. A ⅛-inch-thick spline is used on panel joints. The standard table-saw blade will make a ⅛-inch-wide groove.

groove to begin and end. Usually the spline should be set back from the edge by about one inch.

Next, start the saw. Place the board against the fence and push down on the part of the board that is in front of the saw. This will raise the front of the board off the table. Raise the end of the board enough to clear the blade, and then advance the board until the mark on the board lines up with the mark at the rear of the blade.

Now, slowly lower the board onto the blade. When the board is resting on the table, feed the board through the saw until the second mark on the board lines up with the mark on the fence that is in front of the blade. Hold the board in position and turn off the saw. When the blade stops, remove the board. Then follow the same procedures used to make and assemble the through spline joint.

Splined Frame Joints

A spline can be used to reinforce the joint in a panel door or a drawer dust panel. (A drawer dust panel consists of drawer guides with a solid panel that fills the opening between drawers.) This joint should only be used on plywood or hardboard panel. (Solid-wood panels must not be glued to the frame. They must be able to move in the groove, to allow for shrinkage and swelling. When you use a solid-wood panel, use the mortise-and-tenon joint described in Chapter 9.) A plywood or hardboard panel can be glued into the groove. This adds strength to the door, so a weaker frame joint can be used. A splined frame joint is one of the fastest and easiest ways to make a panel door. (See Illus. 3-6.)

A dado blade should be used on the table saw to make this joint. Set the dado blade to make a ¼-inch-wide groove. Raise the blade until ½ inch extends above the table. Set the fence to center the groove on the edge of the boards. Make a groove on the inside edge of all the frame members. (See Illus. 3-7.) This groove will hold the panel and become part of the corner joint. Cut all of the frame members to exact length after you have made the groove.

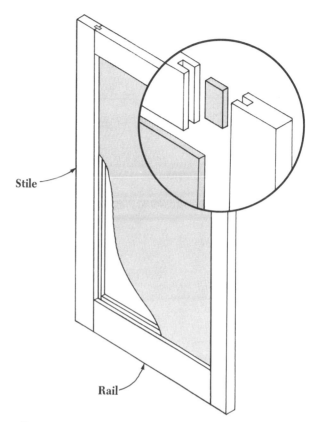

Illus. 3-6. A panel door can be made with spline joints.

Illus. 3-7. To make a door with a splined frame joint, begin by cutting a ¼-inch-wide groove along the inside edge of all the parts.

The next step requires a table-saw accessory called a tenoning jig. Whenever you make a spline groove in the end of a narrow board, use the tenoning jig to hold the board. The tenoning jig firmly clamps the board and guides it across the blade. If you don't use the tenoning jig, a kickback could cause injury.

There are two parts to any frame. The vertical sides are called stiles, and the horizontal board that fits between the stiles is called the rail. Clamp one of the rails in the tenoning jig. Align the jig so that the cut will line up with the groove in the edge of the rail. Turn on the saw and feed the rail across the blade. This will make a groove in the end of the rail. Repeat this procedure for all of the rail ends. (See Illus. 3-8.)

Illus. 3-8. Use a tenoning jig to guide the cut as you make a groove in the end of the rails.

Now, cut a 1-inch-wide spline from ¼-inch-thick hardboard. Cut the spline to length. It can be slightly long, because you can trim the ends after assembly. Begin assembly by applying glue to the joint surfaces of one joint. Put glue in the grooves and spread it around evenly with a small scrap of wood. The strength of the joint depends on a good glue application inside the grooves. Insert the spline into the end of the rail. Align the spline with the groove in the stile, and assemble the joint.

Before assembling the next joint, apply glue to the grooves in the assembled stile and rail and put the panel in place. Finish the assembly of the remaining joints. (See Illus. 3-9.) Be sure to put glue in all of the grooves for the panel. Clamp the joints until the glue sets.

Illus. 3-9. Assembling the panel-door joint.

Using a Router

A router can be used to make the spline grooves. The plunge router is particularly useful for making blind joints. This type of router has a spring-loaded slide mechanism that lets you raise and lower the bit while the router is running. There is also a depth stop that can be set to determine the maximum depth of cut.

Use a bit that will cut a groove of the size needed for the spline. You will need a fence attachment for the router to guide the cut. Set the fence to center the groove on the edge of the board. Adjust the depth of cut to one-half the board thickness. Clamp the work in a vise, or use clamps to secure it to a workbench.

For a through joint, place the router on the work with the fence against the board and the bit close to the edge, but not touching it. Start the router and advance it into the work. Keep the fence against the board as you move the router across to the other edge.

To make a blind joint, set the depth stop on the plunge router to make a groove that is one-half the thickness of the board. Place the router on the work and position the bit over the area where you want the groove to begin. Make sure that the fence is firmly against the board. Start the router and slowly lower the bit into the wood. When the router hits the depth stop, begin to move the router across the board. When you reach the point where the groove should end, stop the router and raise the bit.

Blind Spline Case Joint

A blind spline can be an effective joint for making cabinets. It can be used at a corner or as a T-shaped joint. The plunge router is ideally suited to make blind spline case joints.

Before cutting the grooves, cut the parts to size. Make sure that the cuts are straight and square. Use a table saw or a portable circular saw and a fence or guide board to make the cut. Accuracy at this point will produce a joint that fits together well. The instructions that follow are for ¾-inch-thick boards. The only difference when using thicker boards is that the spline can be thicker and the groove can be deeper.

You will need a plunge router to make a blind joint. Install a ⅛-inch bit in the router. Set the depth of cut to ⅜ inch. Next, set up the router fence to center the groove on the end of the board. Clamp the board, end up. Mark the beginning and end of the groove on the end of the board.

You will be able to see the marks better while cutting the groove if you make marks that show where to stop the router base instead of a mark designating where the bit should stop. To do this, hold the router in position on the board, with the bit over the end of the groove. Make a mark on the end of the board at the edge of the router base. Use a felt-tip pen to make a dark mark that will be visible as you are cutting.

Place the router on the end of the board, with the bit positioned over the location of the beginning of the groove. Make sure that the fence is flat against the side of the board. Start the router and make the plunge cut into the board. Move the router across the board at a steady pace that won't strain the router or cause the bit to burn. (See Illus. 3-10.) When the base lines up with the end mark, stop the router and retract the bit.

The mating groove is made on the face of the other board. For an L-shaped joint, use the same fence setup. Place the board with its inside face up on a bench, and clamp it. Mark the beginning and end of the groove as described above. Place the router on the board with the base on the inside face and the fence against the end. Make the cut as described above. (See Illus. 3-11.)

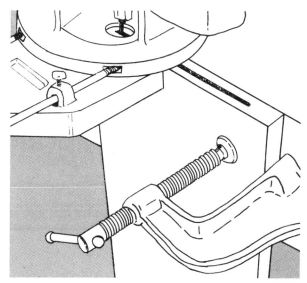

Illus. 3-10. The plunge router can be used to make a blind case joint. A router fence is used to guide the cut. To make the cut on the end of the board, clamp the board to the front of the bench; the outside face of the board should face out. The end of the board should be flush with the bench top, so that the router base will be supported by the bench.

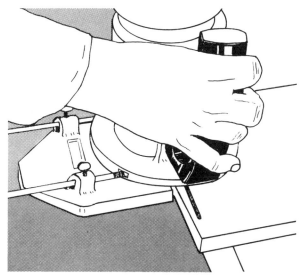

Illus. 3-11. To make the cut on the face of the mating board, clamp the board, with its inside face up, to the bench. Use the same fence setting used to make the first cut.

To make a T-shaped joint, first remove the fence from the router. (See Illus. 3-12.) Draw a line on the board where the groove should be. Place the router on the board near one edge and

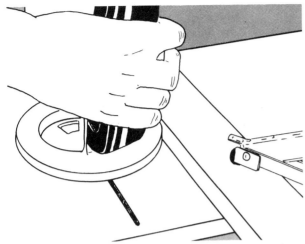

Illus. 3-12. To make the second cut in a T-shaped joint, you must remove the fence. Use a board clamped to the inside face of the board to guide the router.

line up the bit with the layout line. Make a mark on the board at the edge of the router base. Repeat this procedure near the other edge. Place a guide board on the work and line it up with the two marks. Clamp the guide board in place. Mark the ends and make the cut as described above.

Cut a spline from ⅛-inch-thick hardboard. Make the spline ¾ inch wide and cut it to the required length. Apply glue to both joint surfaces and work glue into the groove with a splinter of wood. Insert the spline into one of the grooves. Line up the spline with the second groove and assemble the joint. (See Illus. 3-13.) Clamp the joint until the glue sets.

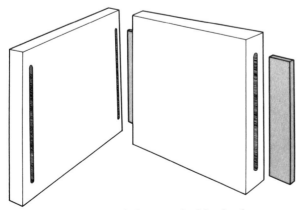

Illus. 3-13. An exploded view of a blind spline case joint.

Using a Plate Joiner

Plate splines are a specialized type of spline. They are made of compressed beech wood. They have an embossed pattern on their surface that gives them a biscuit-like shape and are often called biscuits. Plate splines don't need a continuous groove like standard splines. Instead, they fit into short pockets. (See Illus. 3-14.) The pockets can be cut side by side or end to end, to give additional strength to long joints. A special tool is needed to cut the pocket that the plate splines fit into. This plate-joining tool, sometimes referred to as a biscuit joiner, is basically a plunge-cut circular saw with a 4-inch-diameter blade. (See Illus. 3-15.) Plate-joining is a fast way to make strong joints, so many commercial shops use this method.

The plates come in three sizes. A plate no. 0 is ⅝ inch × 1¾ inches. A no. 10 plate is ¾ inch × 2⅛ inches. A no. 20 plate is 1 inch × 2½ inches. All of the plates are 5⁄32 inch thick. As mentioned, the plates are made from beech wood, and their grain runs diagonally across the spline. This increases the strength of the spline. The plates are

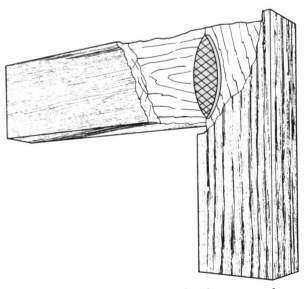

Illus. 3-14. A plate spline is made of compressed beech wood. The grain in the spline runs diagonally across the joint. The embossed pattern helps distribute the glue and grabs the groove as the spline expands. The spline fits into a semi-circular pocket.

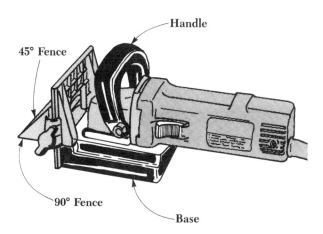

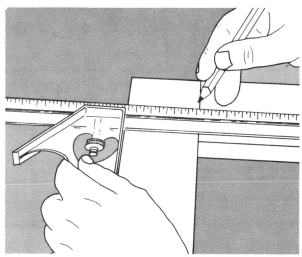

Illus. 3-15. There are many types of plate-joining tools on the market. Most of them operate about the same as this one. A fence is used to guide the cut. The base of some plate-joining tools is used to guide the cut.

Illus. 3-16. To lay out a joint for plate splines, place the parts together the way they should fit after assembly. Use a square to mark across the joint. The plate-joining tool has an index mark that you align with the layout line. You can adjust the joint slightly after assembly, so it is not essential that the index mark be lined up accurately.

compressed when the embossed pattern is pressed in. They will expand when they absorb water. This characteristic ensures that they fit tightly in the pocket.

When you assemble the joint, don't put any glue on the plate. Instead, put glue in the pocket. Once the plate is inserted into the pocket, it will absorb water from the glue and begin to expand.

When you first assemble the joint, the spline will be loose enough to allow you to slide the parts slightly to align them. However, after a few minutes, the plates will swell and wedge tight in the pocket, locking the joint together.

To lay out the plate locations, place the boards together in the same way they will be assembled. Mark one face for reference as you cut the joints. Use a square to mark the plate locations on both boards. (See Illus. 3-16.)

Set the tool for the size of plate spline you will be using. Use the largest plate that will work with the material being used. Set the fence on the plate joiner to center the cut on the board. You will need a flat work surface. Place the first board on the bench with its marked face up. Rest the fence of the plate joiner on the board and press the front of the tool against the edge of the board. Align the index mark on the plate-joiner

base with the mark on the edge of the board. Start the plate joiner and make the cut.

If you are making a frame joint, make one cut on the edge of one board, and the other cut on the end of the other board. Make the cut on the end of the board using the same procedure as described above. (See Illus. 3-17.)

Illus. 3-17. To make the cut for a frame plate spline, place the fence on top of the board and press the base against the end. Push in on the handle to advance the blade into the wood.

After the grooves are cut, apply glue to the joint and insert a plate spline. (See Illus. 3-18.) Line up the spline with the groove in the mating board, and press the joint together. Quickly slide the joint into alignment. If you let the spline swell before the joint is lined up, you won't be able to move the parts. Clamp the joint and let the glue set.

Illus. 3-18. Here you can see how the plate spline fits into the pocket. The pocket is a little longer than the spline, so you can adjust the position of the parts. Make any adjustments quickly, because once the spline begins to swell, the joint is locked in position.

Panel joints can also be made using plate splines. To lay out the joint, place the boards together and mark across both boards at each spline location. If you are just using the splines for alignment purposes, space them far apart. For added strength, place them close together.

Set the fence to center the groove. Place the first board face up on the bench. Rest the plate joiner's fence against the face of the board, and make the cut. After making the first cut, move on to the rest of the pockets, following the same procedure. The cuts in the mating board are made in exactly the same way. Be sure to have its marked face against the fence. (See Illus. 3-19.)

To make an L-shaped case joint, cut the pockets in the end of the first board exactly as described above. Cut the second set of pockets on the face of the mating board. Let the end of the board overhang the edge of the bench slightly when making this cut. Place the fence of the plate-joining tool against the end of the board and make the cut on the inside face.

To make a T-shaped case joint, remove the fence before making the cuts on the face of the board. Clamp a guide board to the work to position the plate joiner. Press the base against the guide board and make the cut on the inside face of the board.

Apply glue to both mating surfaces. Apply a heavy coat of glue to the pockets. Use a splinter or strip of cardboard to spread glue inside the pockets. Insert the plates into one of the joints. Align the joints and assemble them. The pockets are a little longer than the plates. This gives you a small amount of lateral adjustment. If the edges don't line up, slide the parts slightly to get the joint into alignment. Do any adjustment immediately after assembling the joint, because as soon as the plates begin to swell, the joint will be locked in place. Clamp the joint and leave the clamps on until the glue sets.

Illus. 3-19. When making panel joints, either space the cuts close together, as shown here, for maximum strength, or farther apart if they are only needed for alignment during assembly.

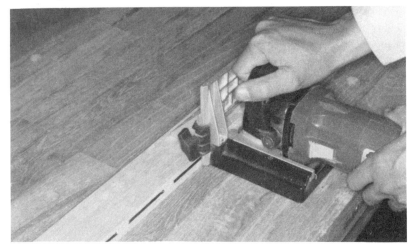

Chapter 4

RABBET JOINTS

A rabbet joint is a corner joint that has one shoulder. (See Illus. 4-1.) It is stronger than a butt joint; however, some type of reinforcement is still needed. Usually, nails or screws are used to reinforce a rabbet. Rabbets are generally used for L-shaped case joints. They can also be used for edge joints. (See Illus. 4-2.) A variation on the rabbet called the shiplap can be used for panel joints.

When to Use a Rabbet

The rabbet joint is one of the most common joints used in cabinetmaking. It can be used to make boxes. It is often used to join the top of a cabinet to its sides, and to attach the back of a cabinet. When the back of a cabinet is placed in a rabbet, the edge of the back panel is completely hidden. A rabbet can be used to join a drawer front to the drawer sides.

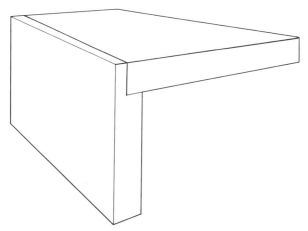

Illus. 4-1. The rabbet joint is a corner joint with one shoulder. It is often used in cabinetmaking.

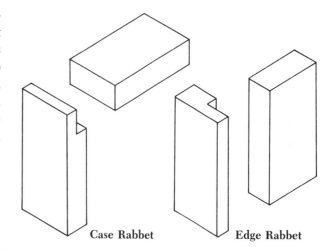

Case Rabbet   Edge Rabbet

Illus. 4-2. The case rabbet joint is used in applications like joining the top of a cabinet to its sides. The edge rabbet can be used to join the back of a cabinet to the sides, or to apply a facing strip to the front of a cabinet or shelf.

Rabbet Variations

You can combine two rabbets in several ways to make variations on the rabbet joint. The shiplap and double rabbet are the two most useful rabbet variations. (See Illus. 4-3.) They are described below.

Shiplap Joint

A shiplap joint is simply two rabbets assembled so that they fit together. It is often used in house siding, but it also has cabinetmaking applications. Panel joints in plywood are usually weak because the plywood edge won't glue well. If you need to join two pieces of plywood together to make a larger piece, use a shiplap joint. The shiplapped boards will give the joint some long-

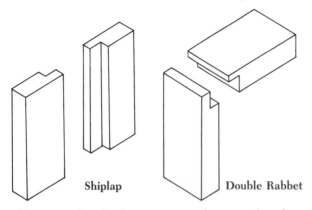

Illus. 4-3. The shiplap joint is used to join the edges of two boards. It can be left unglued to allow for shrinkage and swelling of the boards. The double-rabbet joint has more of a glue surface, giving it greater strength. It can also be used to hide a plywood edge.

grain gluing surface, and make the joint stronger than a butt joint.

A shiplap joint is also used when solid lumber is used to make a cabinet back. The backs of most modern cabinets are made of plywood or hardboard, because a single piece can be used without there being any concern about shrinkage and swelling. The backs of antique reproduction cabinets, however, are made of shiplapped solid wood because this makes the cabinet look more authentic. In this application, the joints are not glued! The shiplap joint allows the boards to shrink and swell with seasonal changes in humidity without affecting the overall size of the back or splitting the boards. The boards are attached with screws. The screws are placed along only one edge of the board. The lip on the adjoining board holds the free edge down while still leaving it free to slide in and out of the joint as seasonal changes occur.

Double-Rabbet Joint

If you cut a rabbet on both boards in a case joint, you will have a double rabbet. The double rabbet increases the glue surface of the joint, adding to its strength. The double rabbet can be used with plywood to hide the plywood edge at the joint. Cut one of the rabbets deeper that usual so that only a very thin piece remains. Cut the second

rabbet in the usual way. When the joint is assembled, the thin projection on the first board covers the edge of the second board. The thin edge that is visible is hardly noticeable.

Making Rabbet Joints

Rabbets can be made using hand tools or several different power tools. Layout is simple. The rabbet should be as wide as the mating board, and its depth should be one-half the thickness of the rabbeted board.

Short rabbets can be made with a hand saw. First, make the shoulder cut in the face of the board. Next, cut in from the end of the board to complete the rabbet. You can make a simple jig that will make it easier to cut accurate rabbets with a hand saw. (This jig is described in the section Using a Handsaw.) Longer rabbets can be made with a special type of plane called a rabbet plane. The rabbet plane procedures are described in the section Using a Rabbet Plane.

Since a good-quality rabbet plane can cost as much as an inexpensive router, most beginners prefer to make rabbets with power tools. Rabbets can be made with a router, a table saw, a radial arm saw, or a jointer. The two most common power tools used are the router and the table saw. Procedures for making rabbets by hand and with a table saw or router are described below.

Using a Handsaw

A simple shop-made jig makes it easy to cut an accurate rabbet joint using a backsaw. (See Illus. 4-4 and 4-5.) The width of the board is limited by the length of the saw. To make the jig, attach a spacer block to the end of a piece of particleboard. A piece of ⅜-inch-thick plywood is just the right thickness for the spacer.

Put the board to be rabbeted on the jig, with the board's inside face up and the end to be rabbeted against the spacer block. Place a ¾-inch-thick guide board that is about 3 inches wide on top of the board and line up its edge with the shoulder line of the rabbet. The guide board can be cut from lumber, plywood, or particleboard.

Illus. 4-4. This jig will help you guide the saw while cutting a rabbet by hand.

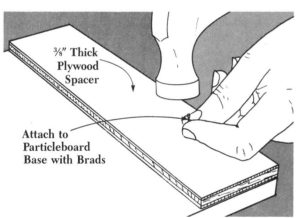

⅜" Thick Plywood Spacer

Attach to Particleboard Base with Brads

Illus. 4-5. This rabbeting jig is simple to make. Its size depends upon the size of the board being rabbeted, and is limited by the length of the saw. Attach a strip of ⅜-inch-thick plywood to the end of a piece of particleboard. This will act as a guide while you make the cheek cut of the rabbet. You will also need a ¾-inch-thick board that is about 3 inches wide to clamp on top of the board you are rabbeting. This board will act as a guide for the saw as you make the shoulder cut.

The important thing is that it has a straight and square edge for the saw to ride against. Use a clamp to hold the guide board down. Place the saw against the guide board and make the shoulder cut. (See Illus. 4-6.) Next, rest the saw on the spacer block and cut into the end of the board to remove the waste from the rabbet. (See Illus. 4-7.) Remove the clamp. The rabbet is completed.

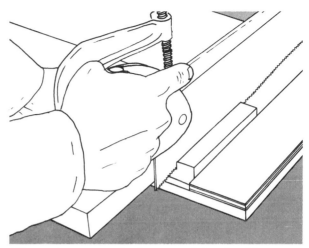

Illus. 4-6. Lay out the location of the shoulder cut on the board. Place the board on the jig with its inside face up. Position the shoulder guide board so that it lines up with the shoulder layout line. Use a C-clamp to clamp the shoulder guide down. The shoulder guide will help you make a straight and square shoulder cut. Rest the side of the saw against the guide as you saw down to the cheek layout line.

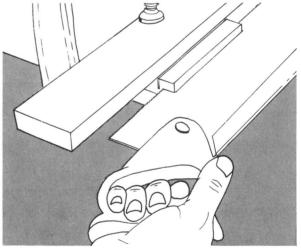

Illus. 4-7. Rest the side of the saw against the guide and make the cheek cut. Stop when you reach the shoulder.

Using a Rabbet Plane

The rabbet plane is constructed so that the blade extends all the way to the outside edges of the plane. There are several types of rabbet plane. Some have a built-in fence to guide the cut, while others require a guide board that is

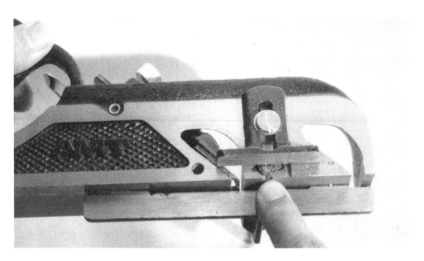

Illus. 4-8. The cutting edge of the plane iron extends all the way to the edge of a rabbet plane. The one shown here has a "nicker." A "nicker" is a sharp spur that severs the wood fibres before the plane iron lifts them. It is used when a cross-grain rabbet is being made. This plane is also equipped with a depth stop and a fence.

clamped to the work to guide the plane. Some planes have a spur that severs the wood fibres along the shoulder of the joint. (See Illus. 4-8.) This makes it possible to cut rabbets across the grain.

To use the rabbet plane to make a rabbet, set the fence and depth stop for the dimensions needed. For short boards, plane along the entire length of the board, and then repeat this procedure until you reach the required depth. (See Illus. 4-9.) For longer boards, plane a short section at a time. Start at the far end of the board so

that the plane will go past the end of the board as you finish the cut. When you have planed down to the depth stop, move back and plane another section, working into the section just finished. When you have planed the rabbet all along the board, make a final pass along the entire length of the board.

Using a Router

A special rabbeting bit is available for the router; it has a pilot that rides against the end of the board and a cutter that will cut the rabbet in a single step. (See Illus. 4-10.) One advantage that

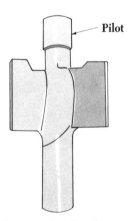

Illus. 4-9. When making a short rabbet with a rabbet plane, you can plane along the entire length of the board in a single pass. For longer boards, start at the end of the board shown here and plane to the depth stop; then step back and plane another section. Finish off with one or two passes along the entire length of the rabbet.

Illus. 4-10. A rabbeting bit for the router has a pilot on its tip that rubs against the edge of the board to guide the cut. The bit shown here is an inexpensive one that has a solid pilot. It works well for most jobs, but if you will be doing a lot of work with a rabbeting bit, use a professional bit that has a ball-bearing pilot.

this type of bit offers is that it can be used to cut rabbets on curved or irregular edges, because the pilot will follow the edge contour.

The size of the bit will determine the width of the rabbet, but the depth of the cut can be adjusted. Set the router depth-of-cut adjustment to make a rabbet that is half the thickness of the board. Clamp the board to a bench with its inside face up. Place the router on the board with the router base on the inside face of the board and the bit pilot close to the edge but past the end of the board, so that you can start the router without having the bit hit the work.

Start the router and advance the bit into the work. Feed the router across the board, keeping the base flat on the face of the board and the pilot against the edge. If the cut is slightly irregular, make another light pass to clean it up.

You can also use a standard straight bit in the router and use a fence to guide the cut. (See Illus. 4-11.) Use a bit that is a little larger than the width of the rabbet. Set the router depth setting to one-half the thickness of the board. Install the router fence and adjust it for the width of the rabbet. Place the router base on the inside face of the board. The fence should be touching the edge of the board. Position the bit so that it is past the end of the board when you start the router.

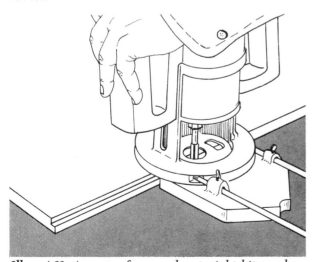

Illus. 4-11. A router fence and a straight bit can be used to make rabbets. Set the router depth for the depth of the rabbet. The fence position controls the width of the cut.

Start the router, and then move the bit into the wood. Cut along the entire length of the board at a steady pace that neither strains the motor nor causes the bit to burn. Make sure that you keep the fence against the edge and the router base flat against the face of the board. If the fence wanders away from the edge, make another pass to clean up the cut.

Using a Table Saw

There are several ways to make a rabbet on the table saw. The simplest method is to use a dado blade. By using the dado blade, you can make the rabbet in one step. Rabbets can be made using the standard blade on the table saw, but it takes two steps. A dado blade is safer and easier for the novice woodworker to use. If you want to try other methods of making rabbets, consult my book on advanced joinery, *Wood Joiner's Handbook*.

To make a rabbet using a dado blade, set the dado blade a little wider than the width of the rabbet. Clamp a scrap board to the table-saw fence. This board protects the blade by keeping it away from the steel fence. Lower the blade beneath the table and slide the fence into position. The distance from the face of the board clamped to the fence to the outside edge of the dado blade should be equal to the width of the rabbet.

Turn on the table saw and slowly raise the blade. The blade will cut into the wood attached to the fence. Raise the blade a little higher than needed, and then turn off the saw. When the blade has stopped, adjust its height so that the rabbet depth will be one-half of the board thickness.

Place the board to be rabbeted on the table saw with its inside face against the table and the edge to be rabbeted against the fence. Turn on the saw and feed the board through. (See Illus. 4-12.) Use a push stick, if necessary, to keep your hands away from the blade.

Assembling a Rabbet

The first step in assembling a rabbet is to apply glue to all of the joint surfaces. Use a small brush

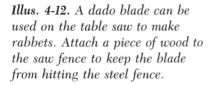

Illus. 4-12. A dado blade can be used on the table saw to make rabbets. Attach a piece of wood to the saw fence to keep the blade from hitting the steel fence.

to spread the glue evenly on the shoulder. Put the boards together and clamp them.

The rabbet is usually an end-grain joint. Since end grain doesn't glue well enough to be relied on for the total strength needed, some type of reinforcement has to be added to the joint. Nails and screws are the most common types of reinforcement used with rabbet joints.

Nails can be driven in from either side. Analyze the stress that will be put on the joint and place the nails at a right angle to the direction of the area that will take the most stress. If you drive them into the shoulder of the joint, angle the nails slightly so that they head towards the center of the rabbeted board. (See Illus. 4-13.)

When appearance is important, use finish nails and set their heads below the surface of the board. Use wood putty to fill in the nail holes. When appearance is not a concern, use box nails, because their heads will make it more difficult to pull the joint apart.

Screws can be used when even more strength is required. Begin by drilling pilot holes. You can use a special bit that drills the pilot and a shank clearance hole and countersinks the head in a single step. (See Illus. 4-14.) You can hide the screw heads with dowel buttons. Set the head below the surface of the board; then put some

glue into the hole and insert a dowel button. Dowel buttons come in several sizes and are available at most hardware stores. (See Illus. 4-15.)

Illus. 4-13. Nails can be driven into the joint from either direction. Here nails are being driven into the shoulder of the joint. This is usually the best way to lock the joint. However, if the joint will withstand more stress in the opposite direction, drive the nails through the cheek. For maximum strength, drive nails in both directions.

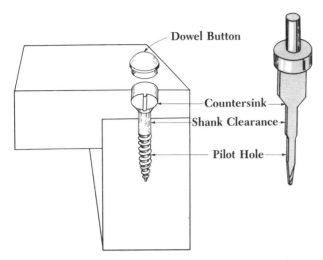

Illus. 4-14. Screws can be used to reinforce a rabbet. In most cases, it is best to drive the screw through the cheek of the joint, since the screw will be too close to the end of the other board if it is driven into the shoulder. Drill a pilot hole before driving a screw. The pilot hole will make it easier to drive the screw, and will prevent splitting. The drill bit shown here is a special type that will drill pilot and shank-clearance holes, and countersink the head in a single step.

Illus. 4-15. Dowel buttons can be used to hide the screw heads. If you will be using dowel buttons, countersink the screw head below the surface of the board just deep enough to get the button in; if you go any deeper, there won't be enough wood left to hold the screw head.

Chapter 5

DADO JOINTS

The dado joint is a T-shaped case joint. (See Illus. 5-1.) Since it has two shoulders, the board is held firmly in place in three directions. The shoulders make it much stronger than a butt joint, and they also help align the joint during assembly. Because there are two shoulders, the joint also helps to prevent the board that fits into the dado from cupping.

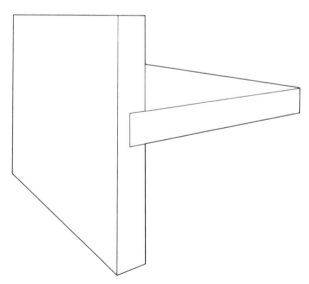

Illus. 5-1. The dado is a T-shaped case joint. It has two shoulders, so the mating board is held firmly in place.

A dado is usually cut to a depth that is one-half the thickness of the board. It is an end-grain joint, so glue alone won't be strong enough for most applications. Dado joints are usually reinforced with nails or screws. They are cut across the grain of the board and are similar to grooves.

Dado Variations

The most common dado variation is the stopped dado. (See Illus. 5-2.) A stopped dado can be used to conceal the joint. The dado stops about ½ inch before reaching the front edge of the board. A notch must be cut in the mating board to fit over the stopped end.

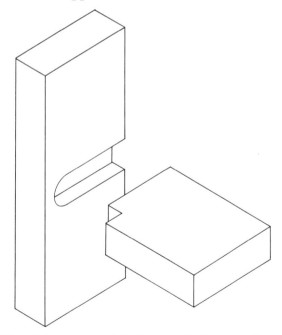

Illus. 5-2. A stopped dado is used when it is desirable to hide the joint. The mating board must be notched to fit over the stopped end.

A sliding dovetail is a dado that has angled shoulders. (See Illus. 5-3.) This locks the joint in a fourth direction so that it cannot be pulled apart. A sliding dovetail is a very strong joint, and no reinforcement is needed. The sliding dovetail shown in Illus. 5-3 can be used for joints up to 12 inches long. Longer joints are too hard to assemble. If you need to use a sliding dovetail for a longer joint, refer to *Wood Joiner's Handbook* for other types of sliding dovetails.

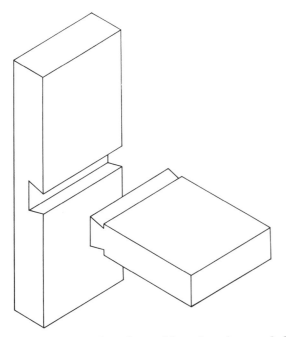

Illus. 5-3. The sliding dovetail has sloped or angled shoulders. The dovetail shape of the joint locks the parts together in all but one direction. The joint can only be assembled or disassembled by sliding the parts together.

When to Use a Dado

A dado joint is most commonly used to attach a shelf to the sides of a cabinet. (See Illus. 5-4.) It is particularly well suited to this application, because the shoulders support the shelf. Dadoes can also be used in drawer construction.

Making Dado Joints

Dadoes can be made with hand or power tools. Short dadoes can be made with a backsaw and a chisel. To cut longer dadoes by hand, a special dado plane is required. The dado plane has two spurs called nickers that cut the wood fibres ahead of the blade. The blade is the width of the dado, and it extends all the way to the sides of the plane. Dado planes are expensive, so most woodworkers today use power tools to make dadoes that are too long to be made with a saw and chisel.

The two most common power tools used to make dadoes are the router and the table saw. To make a dado with a router, all you need are a straight bit and a fence or guide board. For most dadoes, you can get a bit that will cut the dado in one pass. For very wide dadoes, make two or more passes to get the required width. A dado jig

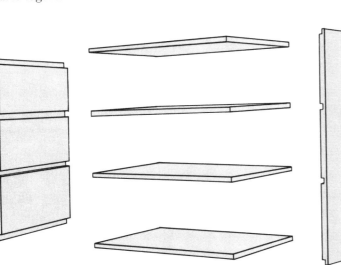

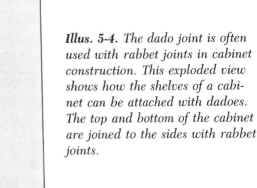

Illus. 5-4. The dado joint is often used with rabbet joints in cabinet construction. This exploded view shows how the shelves of a cabinet can be attached with dadoes. The top and bottom of the cabinet are joined to the sides with rabbet joints.

is a useful accessory that you can make to use with the router. It has a guide board on either side of the router base to prevent the router from moving away from the guide board.

The table saw can be used to make dadoes, if you use an accessory dado blade. Techniques for making dadoes with hand tools and with the table saw and router are explored below.

Using a Handsaw and Chisel

A backsaw and a chisel can be used to make short dadoes. Lay out the joint with a square. Use a backsaw to cut the shoulders. A board clamped to the work can be used to guide the saw. (See Illus. 5-5.) Stop cutting when the saw reaches the bottom of the dado.

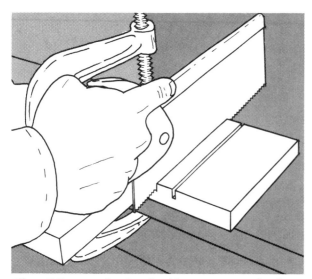

Illus. 5-5. To make the shoulder cuts, use a backsaw. A board clamped to the work can be used to guide the saw and keep it square with the face of the board.

Use a chisel to remove the waste between the saw kerfs. Make large cuts at first to remove most of the wood. (See Illus. 5-6.) Smooth the bottom of the dado with the chisel.

Using a Router

To make a dado with a router, you need a straight bit that is the right size for the dado being made and a guide for the router. If the dado is close to the end of the board, you can use a router fence

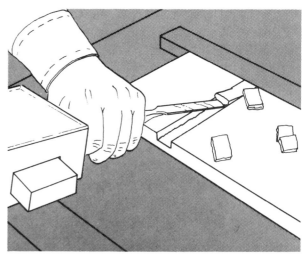

Illus. 5-6. Use a chisel to remove the waste between the two shoulder cuts.

to guide the cut. Usually, the dado will be too far away from the end for you to use a router fence. In this case, clamp a guide board to the work. The router base rubs against the guide board. The only problem with using a guide board is that if the router wanders away from the board, the joint is ruined. You can make a simple jig that guides the router on both sides, so there is no possibility of the router wandering off course. (See Illus. 5-7.)

The jig is simple to make. It consists of ⅛-inch-thick hardboard and some strips of plywood or particleboard. The jig can be made to any length needed. Attach one strip to the hardboard with glue and nails. Now, place the router near one end of the jig with the base against the strip. Make a mark indicating the opposite edge of the router base. Move the router to the opposite end of the jig and make another mark.

Now, line up the next strip with these marks and attach it to the hardboard with glue and nails. Cut two short pieces to fill in the ends between the two strips, and glue and nail them in place.

Next, place the router in the jig. It should be able to slide freely along the length of the jig. Support the jig on blocks at either end, and clamp it to a bench.

Put a straight bit in the router and place the router on the jig. With the router at one end of

Illus. 5-7. This dado jig guides the router on both sides so that it can't wander. You can make this jig yourself to any size needed.

the jig, make a plunge cut through the hardboard base. Rout a slot in the hardboard along the length of the jig. The dado jig is now ready to use.

Lay out the position of the dado, and then line up the jig with the layout marks on the board. Clamp the jig in place. Put a straight bit in the router. Use a bit that will cut the desired width of the dado. Set the depth of cut to one-half the board thickness.

Place the router on the jig with the bit past the edge of the board. Start the router and advance the bit into the wood. Cut across the board, feeding the router at a rate that doesn't strain the motor or cause the bit to burn. For most dadoes, continue the cut all the way across the board.

The router is a very good tool to use to make a stopped dado. Simply make a mark on the jig where you want the router base to be when the cut should stop. Then, when you reach the mark, stop the router and lift it off the jig.

Using a Table Saw

To make dadoes on the table saw, you will need a dado blade. There are two types of dado blades: stack dado and wobble blades. The stack dado blade is a set of two blades and several chippers. (See Illus. 5-8.) The chippers are of various thicknesses. The width of the dado is determined by the combination of chippers placed between the blades.

The wobble dado blade consists of a single blade that wobbles back and forth to create a kerf that is wider than the blade. (See Illus. 5-9.) A twin-blade wobbler is also available. The two blades are angled together in a V shape. The amount of wobble is adjustable. There is a scale on the blade assembly to indicate the width of

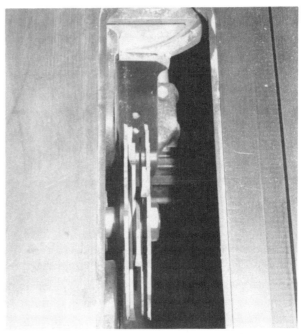

Illus. 5-8. The stack dado blade consists of two saw blades separated by several chippers. The chippers are of different thicknesses. By varying the number and size of the chippers, you can adjust the width of the dado.

Illus. 5-10. To adjust the wobble blade, twist the center hub until the index mark lines up with the desired measurement on the scale.

Illus. 5-9. The wobble dado blade uses a single blade. The blade is set at an angle to the arbor. The width of the dado is adjusted by changing the angle of the blade.

the dado. You rotate part of the blade assembly until the desired width is aligned with an index mark. (See Illus. 5-10.)

Once they are set up, the procedure for using the two types of blades is the same. Set the dado blade to the required width. Use a special table insert that will accommodate the wide cut. Raise the blade to the depth of cut required.

For short dadoes, use the mitre gauge to guide the board. With the saw turned off, line up the layout marks on the edge of the board with the blade. Then pull the board back away from the blade and start the saw. Feed the board into the blade.

For longer dadoes, use the rip fence to guide the cut. (See Illus. 5-11.) Set the fence for the correct distance. Place the edge of the board against the fence and feed the work into the blade. Make sure that you keep your fingers well away from the blade. The blade will be hidden during the cut, so be sure you know where it is. If you have your hand in line with the blade, you can be injured as the board exits the saw.

Illus. 5-11. When working with large boards, use the rip fence to guide the cut.

Assembling Dado Joints

Use glue and nails or screws to assemble dado joints. Bar clamps are helpful when assembling a project, but they are not absolutely necessary when you use nails or screws to pull the joint tight.

Begin by applying glue to the joint. Spread an even coat of glue on both shoulders and the bottom of the joint. (See Illus. 5-12.) Line up the mating boards with the dado and assemble the joint. If the board is cupped slightly, you can pull it straight by inserting one corner of the board into the dado and working the rest of the board in as you bend the cupped section. Use clamps to hold the joint tight as you add screws or nails.

To reinforce with screws, first drill a pilot hole in the board from its outside face and then drive the screws into the joint. The screw heads can be hidden with dowel buttons. (See Illus. 5-13.)

Nails can also be used. Drive the nail in from the outside face. Finish nails can be set, and the holes hidden with wood putty.

Nails or screws can be concealed by driving them in on an angle from the inside of the joint. Be careful not to let their points break through to the outside face. (See Illus. 5-14.) Use a drill bit that will countersink the screw head when you drill the pilot hole at an angle. The bit will make a pocket for the screw head. (See Illus. 5-15.) After assembly, fill the pocket with wood putty.

After the joint has been reinforced with nails or screws, remove the clamps.

Sliding Dovetails

The sliding dovetail can be used in most applications where a standard dado would be used. By

Illus. 5-13. If you countersink the screw heads below the surface of the board, you can hide them with dowel buttons.

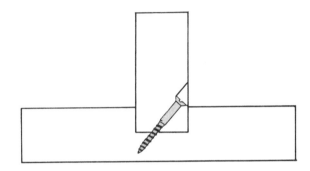

Illus. 5-14. Another way to conceal screws is to install them at an angle from inside the joint.

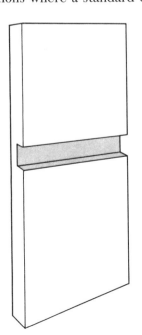

Illus. 5-12. Before assembly, apply glue to both shoulders and the bottom of the dado (the shaded area).

Illus. 5-15. Drill angled pilot holes before installing the screws. Use the type of drill bit that has a built-in countersink. Countersink the hole deep enough to make a pocket for the screw head. After the screws are installed, fill the pocket with wood putty.

Illus. 5-16. The sliding dovetail can be made with a router. The angled shoulders lock the joint, so screws or nails are not needed.

using the sliding dovetail, you can eliminate the need for nails or screws. The joint can only be disassembled by sliding out of the dado, so it is very strong. (See Illus. 5-16.)

To make a sliding dovetail joint, you will need a router and a dovetail bit. Place a dovetail bit in the router. Set the depth of cut to the required depth of the dado. Set up the dado jig as you would for a normal dado. Clamp it in place. Make the cut as you would a normal dado. (See Illus. 5-17.)

Illus. 5-17. You can use the same dado jig to make sliding dovetails. The procedure for making a sliding dovetail is the same as for making a standard dado, except that you use a dovetail bit in the router.

The end of the mating board must be cut to fit the dovetailed dado. Make a test cut first on a scrap board. Clamp the board to the front of a bench, with the end of the board flush with the top of the bench. Place the dado jig on top of the bench, with its slot over the edge of the board. The slot should be past the board so that just the inside edge lines up with the outside edge of the board.

Clamp the jig firmly to the bench. Make a cut across the board using this jig setup. The depth of cut for the router should be left at the same setting used to cut the dado. (See Illus. 5-18.) Turn the board around and follow the same procedure to make another cut on the opposite face of the board.

Illus. 5-18. To make the cuts on the mating board, clamp the board to the front of the bench. The end of the board should be flush with the top of the bench. Place the dado jig on the bench, with its slot overhanging the board.

Check the fit of the test board in the dovetail's dado. It will probably be too big. Move the jig the distance needed to bring the cut into the proper location, and reclamp the jig. Make another pass over the work. If the cut is in the proper location, make a note of the required offset for future use. When you are satisfied with the fit, make the cuts on the actual boards for the project.

To assemble the joint, apply glue to the mating surfaces. A small brush makes it easier to spread the glue around inside the dado. Slide the joint together quickly before the glue binds the surfaces. No clamping is necessary.

Chapter 6

TONGUE-AND-GROOVE JOINTS

The tongue-and-groove joint is made up of two parts. The *tongue* is a projection on one board that fits into the *groove* on the mating board. (See Illus. 6-1.) In most cases, the width of the tongue and groove is equal to one-third the thickness of the board, and the depth of the groove is equal to one-half the thickness of the board. The tongue-and-groove joint is primarily used as a panel joint, but it can also be used as a case joint.

Tongue-and-Groove Variations

There are two variations on the tongue-and-groove joint that are very useful in cabinetmaking. The first is the case tongue-and-groove joint. (See Illus. 6-2.) This is a T-shaped joint. It can be

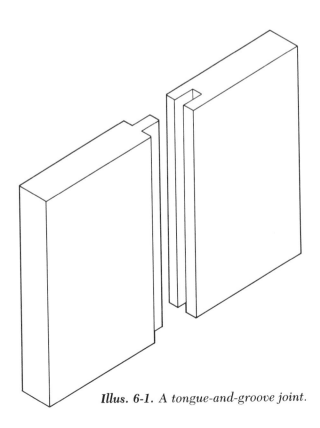

Illus. **6-1.** *A tongue-and-groove joint.*

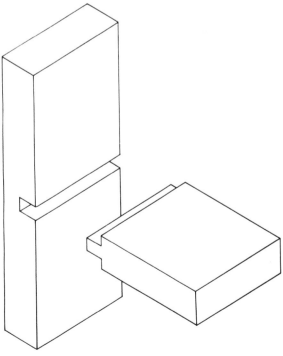

Illus. **6-2.** *The case tongue-and-groove joint can be used in cabinetmaking.*

used like a dado, but the shoulders on the tongue help to hide any splintering or imperfections in the groove. This joint can be made blind when it is desirable to hide it.

The barefaced tongue-and-groove joint is an L-shaped case joint. (See Illus. 6-3.) It can be used in the same applications as a rabbet, but is much stronger than a rabbet. The barefaced tongue-and-groove joint is really just a dado and a rabbet combined into one joint. To make this joint, just cut a rabbet on the end of one board, and then make a dado in the mating board that will fit the rabbet (tongue) made on the first board.

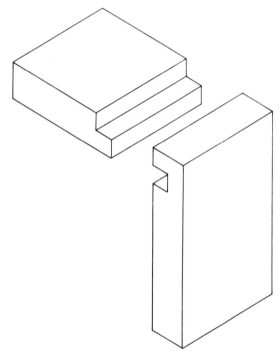

Illus. 6-3. The barefaced tongue-and-groove joint is used near the end of the board. Using a barefaced tongue places the groove farther away from the end of the board, so there is less chance of the joint breaking.

Illus. 6-4 (right). When a number of boards need to be joined together into a large panel such as the back of this cabinet, the tongue-and-groove joint is a good joint to use. The joints are not glued, so the boards can shrink and swell with changes in humidity.

When to Use a Tongue-and-Groove Joint

A tongue-and-groove joint can be used whenever you need a large panel of solid lumber, as, for example, the back of a traditional cabinet. (See Illus. 6-4.) The back can be made of many narrow boards tongue and grooved together. Each board

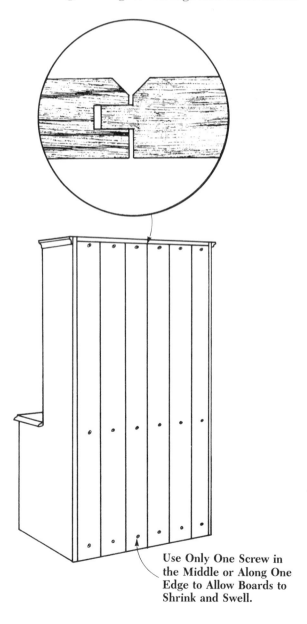

Use Only One Screw in the Middle or Along One Edge to Allow Boards to Shrink and Swell.

is screwed to the cabinet in the center or along one edge, and the other edge is left free. No glue is used in the joint. Sometimes a bevel or a bead is used at each joint to make the joint more decorative.

When used as a panel joint, the tongue-and-groove joint is usually not glued. One of the main advantages of this joint is that it will hold boards together while still allowing some movement when seasonal shrinkage and swelling occurs.

Tongue-and-groove boards are often used for siding and wall panelling. Each board is screwed or nailed to the supports along one edge or in the middle. The rest of the board is free to move. As the board shrinks, the tongue pulls out of the groove slightly, but there is still enough left in the groove to hold the joint together. If the boards were solidly attached to each other, the boards would split as they shrank, because there would be no room for movement.

A tongue-and-groove joint can also be used to make a panel door. The solid-wood panel must be free to move in the frame, or it will split or break the frame joints. A tongue on all four sides of the panel fits into a groove in the frame. This is an example of cross-grain construction, in which one part runs at a right angle to the grain in the other part. When it is used in cross-grain construction, the tongue-and-groove joint is not glued, allowing freedom of movement that will prevent split boards and broken joints. This same technique can be used to frame other large panels. For example, if you want to make a headboard for a bed that has a large, solid-wood panel, you can use a tongue-and-groove joint to attach the panel to the posts.

The case tongue-and-groove joint can be used to build cabinets. Blind joints can be used to conceal the joint. The tongue-and-groove joint can be used in place of dadoes to attach the shelves and other parts.

The tongue-and-groove joint has several advantages. The shoulders on the tongue add strength to the joint. This joint is particularly useful when plywood is being used, because any chipping that occurs along the groove as you cut it will be hidden by the shoulders on the tongue.

You can sand the parts heavily after milling without fear of loosening the joint. If you sand the parts of a dado after the joint is cut, you run the risk of a loose joint, because the board will be thinner than it was when you cut the dado.

Making Tongue-and-Groove Joints

Tongue-and-groove joints traditionally were made with a set of matched planes. One plane has a blade shaped to cut a tongue; another plane, the matching one, has a blade to cut a groove. Using planes can be fun, but they are hard to find and expensive, so most woodworkers today use power tools to make a tongue-and-groove joint.

The fastest way to make a tongue-and-groove joint is to use a shaper with a matched set of tongue-and-groove cutters. (See Illus. 6-5.) This is the method production shops use to make tongue-and-groove joints. One cutter makes a tongue, and the second cutter makes a matching groove. Since most beginning woodworkers won't have a shaper, I'll describe two other methods that use more common power tools: the router and the table saw.

Using a Table Saw

The most efficient way to make tongue-and-groove joints with the table saw is to use a moulding head on the saw. This is an attachment that fits on the arbor in place of a blade. Replaceable cutters fit into slots in the head. You can get cutters that will cut the tongue and groove like the shaper cutters.

If you don't want to get a moulding head, use a dado blade to make tongue-and-groove joints. The groove is made in one pass. The tongue takes two passes. When two passes are made, the result is a rabbet on each side of the board, which leaves a tongue in the middle.

Before making the joints, lay out the panel and cut the boards to their widths. Joint the edges to

Illus. 6-5. This shaper cutter is used to make a groove. A matching cutter is used to make a tongue. The shaper is one of the most efficient ways to make a tongue-and-groove joint.

get a straight, true edge. Now, use the table saw to cut the groove. Install the dado blade; then set the width of the groove to one-third the width of the board. Raise the blade height to one-half the thickness of the board. Set the table-saw fence to center the groove on the edge of the board.

Turn on the saw and feed the board through, with its edge against the table and one face against the fence. Cut a groove on one edge of all of the boards needed to make up the panel. (See Illus. 6-6.)

Now, set up the saw to cut the tongue. Add a wood auxiliary fence to the steel fence. Lower the blade below the table and position the wood

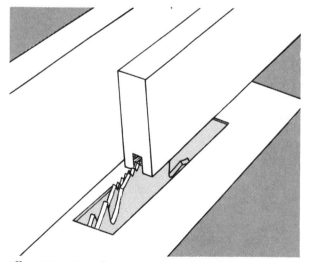

Illus. 6-6. To make a groove on the table saw, install the dado blade and adjust it to one-third the width of the board. Raise the blade to one-half the thickness of the board. Set the fence to center the cut.

fence so that it is slightly over the blade. Turn on the saw and raise the blade to cut a pocket in the wood fence.

Turn off the saw and reposition the fence to make a rabbet. Mark the size of the tongue on the end of the board and use it to adjust the position of the fence and the blade height.

Make a test cut on a scrap board. Place the face of the board against the fence and the edge on the table. Make the cut on one side, and then turn the board around and make the cut on the other side. (See Illus. 6-7.) You can also make the tongue with the face of the board on the table and its edge against the fence. This setup is better when the board is large and would be hard to handle on its edge.

Place the test tongue in the groove and see how it fits. (See Illus. 6-8.) It should slide in snugly, but should not fit overly tight. If you need to adjust the fit, raise or lower the blade height or adjust the fence position. Make very small adjustments, because the effect will be doubled. Now, make the tongues on all of the boards.

Using a Router

There are two ways to make a tongue-and-groove joint with a router. You can buy a set of matched bits similar to the type used on the shaper. This is an efficient way to make the joint, if you will be making a lot of them; but if you will only use the joint occasionally, you use a straight bit to make

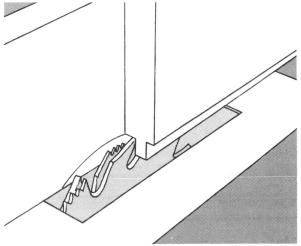

Illus. 6-7. It takes two passes over the table saw to make a tongue. A wood auxiliary fence is needed to keep the blade from hitting the steel saw fence.

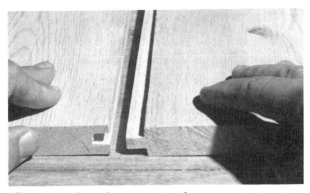

Illus. 6-8. Place the tongue in the groove to test its fit. The tongue should fit snugly in the groove without being too tight.

it. This method is somewhat slower, but it works well. The groove is made in one step, but the tongue takes two steps. The straight bit is used to cut a rabbet on each side of the board, forming the tongue.

The blind tongue-and-groove joint can be used to attach shelves to the sides of cabinets or similar applications. The router is the best way to make a blind groove. Place a straight bit in the router. For ¾-inch-thick boards, a ¼- or ³⁄₁₆-inch bit works well. Set the depth of cut to one-half the thickness of the board.

The joint is usually too far from the end of the board for the router fence to be used, so use the dado jig described in Chapter 5 to guide the router. Place the jig in position on the board. Position the end of the jig so that it will stop the router one inch away from the edge of the board. Clamp the jig in place.

Place the router in the jig with the bit past the rear edge of the board. Start the router and cut the groove across the board. (See Illus. 6-9.) When the router base hits the end of the jig, stop the router and lift it off. Repeat this procedure for all of the other grooves in the project.

Now, set up to make the tongues. Make a test cut on scrap wood first. Clamp the board to the front of a bench with the end of the board flush with the bench top. Install a fence on the router. Use the same straight bit you used to make the groove. Set the depth of cut and the router fence

Illus. 6-9. To cut a groove in the face of a board, use the dado jig described in Chapter 5. You are actually cutting a narrow dado, but it is called a groove in this application.

so that the tongue will fit in the groove. Make a pass across the board; then unclamp the board, turn it around, and make another cut on the other side. (See Illus. 6-10.)

Test the fit in the groove. Make any necessary adjustment before you make the cuts on the actual board for the project. (See Illus. 6-11.) When you are satisfied with the fit, cut the tongue on all of the boards in the project.

If you want the board with the tongue to be flush with the front edge of the other board, trim the tongue near the front edge of the board. Use a backsaw to cut away one inch of the tongue at the front of the joint.

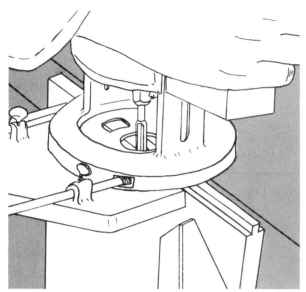

Illus. 6-10. To cut the tongue with a router, clamp the board to the front of the bench. The end of the board should be flush with the bench top. Use a router fence to guide the cut. Keep the router base flat against the bench top as you make the cut. If you are using plywood, it is a good idea to make a light pass across the face of the board first, before making the final cut. This will help to minimize chipping.

Illus. 6-11. Test the fit of the sample tongue in the groove. Make the necessary adjustments before cutting the tongues on the project boards.

Chapter 7

LAP JOINTS

Lap joints are primarily frame joints. The strength of a lap joint comes from the large amount of long-grain glue surface and the shoulders. Glue alone will hold a lap joint together. Sometimes a few small nails are used to hold the joint together while the glue dries, but they are not needed for added strength.

Lap joints can be used at a corner, or on T-shaped or cross joints. (See Illus. 7-1.) T-shaped and cross lap joints are even stronger than corner lap joints because of the additional shoulders that help counteract twisting forces.

In most cases, the lap is cut halfway through the board, resulting in a flush joint. These joints are called half-laps. Since much of the strength comes from the glue bond between the two cheeks, clamps should be used to press the cheeks tightly together. Once the joint has been clamped, you either can drive a few nails through it and remove the clamp or omit the

nails and leave the clamp in place until the glue sets.

When to Use Lap Joints

Lap joints are used to make all kinds of frames. They can be used to make cabinet face frames. They also can be used to make door frames, particularly if a plywood panel is used inside the frame. The panel is glued into a rabbet cut into the back of the frame. For solid-wood panels, use the mortise-and-tenon joint, which is described in Chapter 9. Variations on the lap joint can be used where the stretchers between table legs cross, or when making small knockdown bookcases from plywood.

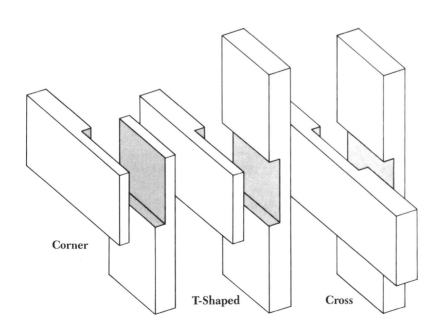

Corner

T-Shaped   **Cross**

Illus. 7-1. Lap joints can be used at a corner or when the parts cross or meet in a T-shaped joint.

Lap-Joint Variations

There are a number of variations on the half-lap joint. You can cut the shoulders on an angle to make a *dovetailed half-lap*. (See Illus. 7-2.) This joint has extra strength because it is locked in another direction.

Half-laps can be cut at angles other than 90 degrees. You can make odd-shaped frames easily using half-laps. (See Illus. 7-3.) To lay out an angled half-lap, simply place the parts in position with one board overlapping the other; then use the edges of the boards to draw layout lines on the mating board. When using a handsaw, just place the saw on the layout line. If using the table saw, adjust the mitre gauge to the appropriate angle.

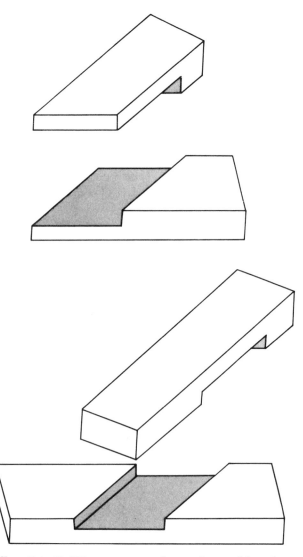

Illus. 7-3. Half-lap joints can be made at odd angles when necessary.

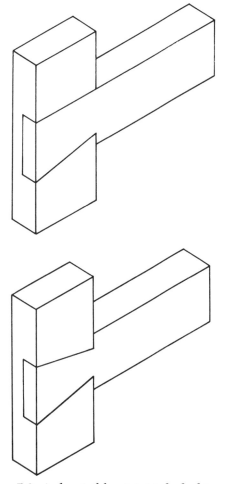

Illus. 7-2. A dovetail lap joint is locked together.

Bridle joints are used when the end of one board meets the edge of another. (See Illus. 7-4.) A bridle joint is often used to attach a rocker to the legs of a rocking chair. When the boards are the same thickness, you must notch out both sides of the board that fits into the bridle. The procedure is similar to making a T-shaped half-lap, but the cut is only one-third the width of the board. When the board with the bridle is thicker than the other board, a barefaced bridle joint can be used.

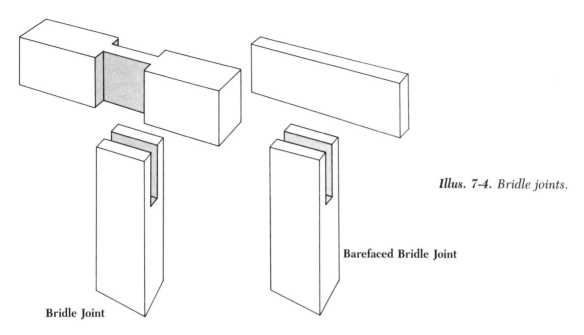

Illus. 7-4. Bridle joints.

Barefaced Bridle Joint

Bridle Joint

Edge half-laps are used when two frame members must cross on an edge. Edge half-laps are used on X-shaped stretchers between table legs. The simplest type of edge half-lap is made by cutting a notch halfway through each board where they meet. (See Illus. 7-5.) This works fine on narrow boards or on boards where strength is not a major factor. When more strength is needed, a *dadoed half-lap* can be used. (See Illus. 7-6.) The dadoed-edge half-lap supports the edges of the joint with small shoulders. This im-

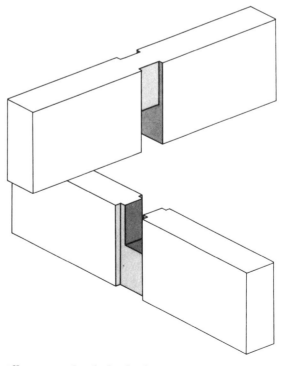

Illus. 7-6. The dadoed-edge cross-lap adds support to the joint so that there is less chance for breakage along the grain.

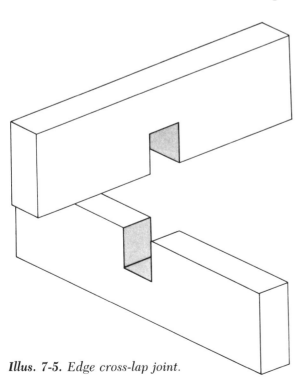

Illus. 7-5. Edge cross-lap joint.

proves the strength of the joint and helps to prevent breaks along the grain that can develop when wide boards are joined with edge half-laps.

An *unsupported-edge lap joint* can be used with plywood, because the alternating grain of the plywood makes it less likely that the unsupported area will break off. Long, unsupported half-laps are often used to make knockdown furniture such as bookcases and small tables that can be assembled and disassembled easily. The parts simply slide together. (See Illus. 7-7.)

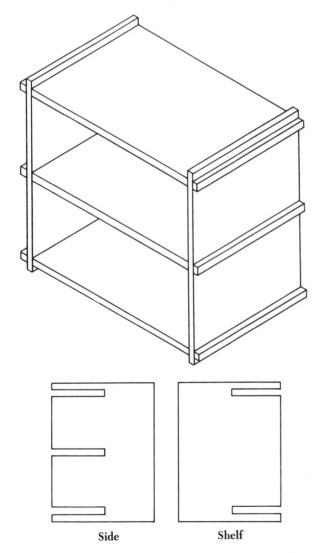

Illus. 7-7. Long, unsupported-edge lap joints can be used with plywood. This type of joint is often used to make knockdown furniture such as this bookcase. The shelves slide into the notches in the sides.

Making Half-Laps

Half-laps can be made with hand or power tools. This is one of the easiest joints to make with hand tools, so it is often used when power equipment is not available. All you need to make a corner half-lap is a backsaw. You will need a saw and a chisel to make the T-shaped or cross half-lap joint.

The following sections describe how to make different types of half-lap joints by hand and with a table saw and router.

Making Corner Half-Laps with a Backsaw

The corner half-lap joint can be cut entirely with a backsaw. This is one of the easiest joints to cut by hand. (See Illus. 7-8.) The following method of making corner half-lap joints has an advantage in that you can always see both layout lines that you are following. If you simply cut straight down the cheek, you can't see the line on the opposite edge of the board; so the saw can stray from that line, leaving an angled cheek.

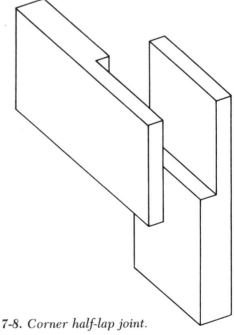

Illus. 7-8. Corner half-lap joint.

Begin by laying out the joint. Lay the boards on top of each other to mark the location of the shoulder cut; then make the shoulder mark with a sharp knife. Use a square to guide the knife. Using a knife to make the mark helps you to get a clean shoulder cut. The knife will cut the wood fibres, so there won't be much splintering along the saw cut. (See Illus. 7-9.) Use the square to transfer the shoulder mark to the edges.

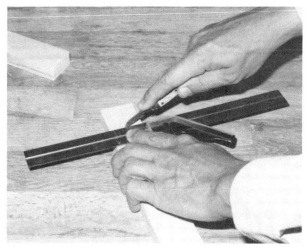

Illus. 7-9. Mark the shoulder with a knife.

Set a marking gauge to one-half the thickness of the board, and mark both edges and the end. (See Illus. 7-10.) Then place the first board in the vise with its end up and the board at about a 45-

Illus. 7-10. Set the marking gauge for one-half the thickness of the board, and mark the end and both edges of the board.

degree angle. Place the saw on the end of the board so that the kerf (the cut) will be entirely on the waste side of the line. Use your thumb to steady the saw as you start the cut. Cut down about ⅛ inch. (See Illus. 7-11.)

Illus. 7-11. Start the cut with the saw flat against the end of the board.

Now, change the saw's position so that it is parallel to the bench. With the saw in this position, you can see how it is lined up with the layout lines on the end and one edge of the board. Saw down both lines until the saw reaches the shoulder mark. (See Illus. 7-12.)

Take the board out of the vise and turn it around. Reclamp it at about a 45-degree angle like before, but this time with the opposite face out. Place the saw in the kerf that is already cut in the end of the board. Start sawing; while sawing, lower the saw handle until the saw is parallel with the bench. Saw down until you reach the shoulder mark.

Illus. 7-12. Follow the layout line as you saw down the shoulder mark.

Reposition the board in the vise so that it is straight up and down. Place the saw in the kerf and cut straight down until you reach the shoulder mark. (See Illus. 7-13.)

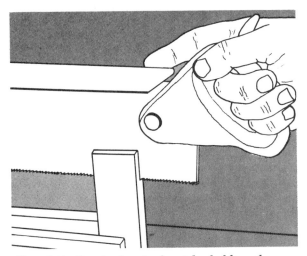

Illus. 7-13. Finish the cheek cut by holding the saw parallel to the shoulder line and cutting straight down.

Remove the board from the vise and place it in a mitre box. Cut straight down the shoulder mark until the waste is free. (See Illus. 7-14.) Repeat the same procedure for the other board.

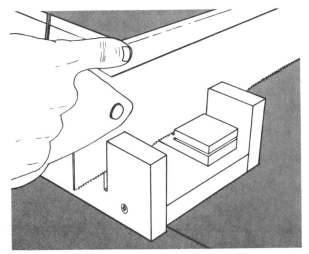

Illus. 7-14. Make the shoulder cut in a mitre box.

Apply glue to both mating parts of the joint. Spread the glue evenly over the cheek and shoulder. Assemble the joint and clamp it. Place the clamps so that the cheeks are firmly pressed together. You can leave the clamps on until the glue sets, or you can drive a few nails into the joint and remove the clamps.

Making T-Shaped and Cross-Lap Joints with a Backsaw and Chisel

To make T-shaped and cross-lap joints, you must use a chisel and a backsaw. Lay out the joint by placing the parts on top of each other in the correct orientation. Mark the shoulders. One of the parts on a T-shaped joint is just like the parts on a corner half-lap. (See Illus. 7-15.) Lay it out and cut it following the directions above.

The other part of the T-shaped joint and both parts of a cross-lap joint have two shoulders. Finish the layout by transferring the shoulder marks to the edges with a square, and then use a marking gauge set to one-half the thickness of the board to mark the cheek.

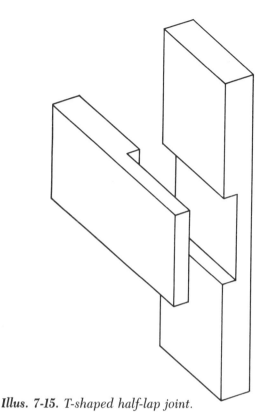

Illus. 7-15. T-shaped half-lap joint.

Place the board in a mitre box. Cut the shoulders, keeping the saw kerf entirely in the waste. Make additional cuts in the waste about every ½ inch. Stop the cuts when they reach the cheek mark. (See Illus. 7-16.)

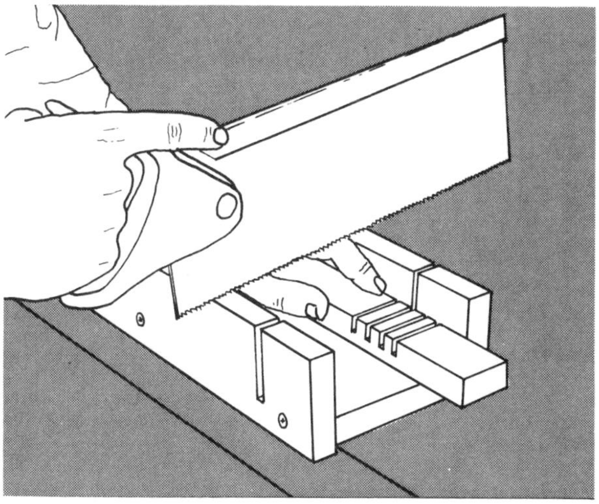

Illus. 7-16. Make several saw cuts in the waste area to make it easier to remove the waste with a chisel.

Now, use a chisel to remove the waste. Hold the chisel bevel-side down to make the rough cut that will remove most of the waste. Turn the chisel bevel-side up and pare the cheek until it is smooth and level with the layout lines. (See Illus. 7-17.)

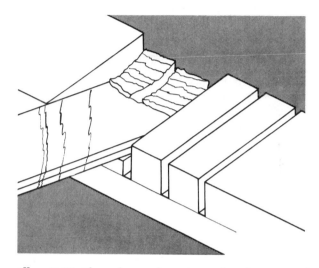

Illus. 7-17. Place the work against a bench stop, and chisel out the waste between the shoulder cuts.

Making Corner Half-Laps with a Table Saw

You can use a standard blade and a tenoning jig on a table saw to make a corner half-lap joint. The procedure is the same as the one used to make a tenon with the tenoning jig. (See Chapter 9.)

Set up the tenoning jig so that you can clamp the part vertically. Adjust the jig to make the cheek cut. Make sure that all of the saw kerf will be on the waste side of the line. Clamp the board to the jig and make the cut. (See Illus. 7-18.) Then remove the board from the tenoning jig and use the mitre gauge to guide the shoulder cut.

Clamp a block of wood to the saw fence to act as a positioning guide. Adjust the fence so that when the end of the board is butted against the stop, it will be in the correct position to make the shoulder cut. Adjust the blade height to one-half the thickness of the board.

Illus. 7-18. A tenoning jig is used to make the cheek cut. It will hold the board securely in the vertical position, so that you can make the cut safely.

Place the board face down on the saw. The board's edge should be against the mitre gauge. Butt the end against the stop. Hold the board firmly in position on the mitre gauge as you slide the gauge forward. The end of the board should clear the stop before the cut begins. (See Illus. 7-19.) If the end of the board is in contact with the stop or the fence while you make the cut, there is a danger that the waste may kick back; so be sure to follow the procedure correctly.

Stop Block

Mitre Gauge

Illus. 7-19. Use the mitre gauge to guide the shoulder cut. Use a stop block clamped to the fence to position the board.

A dado blade can be used to cut all types of lap joints, including the T-shaped and cross-lap joints that can't be made with the tenoning jig. Install the dado blade on the saw and set it to its widest setting. Raise the blade to one-half the thickness of the board. Use the mitre gauge to guide the work. You can line up on the shoulder mark visually or set a stop with the fence. To use the fence as a stop, clamp a board to the front end of the fence. Move the fence until the distance between the edge of the board on the fence and the far side of the blade is equal to the distance from the end of the board to the shoulder.

Place the board against the mitre gauge and butt the end of the board against the stop. Hold the board firmly in position against the mitre gauge as you slide it past the stop and begin cutting. (See Illus. 7-20.)

Illus. 7-20. Using a dado blade to make a half-lap joint. A stop block clamped to the fence can be used to position the board for the shoulder cut.

After making the shoulder, lift the board off and pull the mitre gauge back. Reposition the board on the mitre gauge so that the next cut will just slightly overlap the first; then advance the work into the blade again and make another pass. Continue in this manner until all of the waste has been removed. (See Illus. 7-21.) For a corner half-lap, repeat this procedure on the other board.

Illus. 7-21. After making the shoulder cut, reposition the board and remove the waste.

For T-shaped and cross-lap joints, the procedure is similar, except you must make a second shoulder cut. After both shoulders are cut, remove the waste by making additional passes across the blade. (See Illus. 7-22.)

Making Half-Lap Joints with a Router

All types of half-lap joints can be made with the router. The cut will be smoother than those made with a dado blade, but the setup and cutting are

Illus. 7-22. The dado blade is an ideal way to make T-shaped and cross lap joints.

more time-consuming. Install a straight bit in the router. Set the depth of cut to one-half the thickness of the board.

Place the board on a bench and put scrap boards of equal thickness on either side of the board; then clamp a guide board across the boards to act as a stop for the shoulder cut. The guide-board position is determined by the diameter of the router base. Place the router on the work, and line up the bit with the shoulder mark. Butt the guide board against the router base and use a square to position it. Clamp the guide board in place.

Place the router on the work with the bit extending past the end of the board far enough so that it won't hit the wood when you turn on the router. Start the router and advance it into the end of the board. Work back and forth, making a cut that doesn't strain the router, until the base hits the guide board. Make a smooth cut across the shoulder. (See Illus. 7-23.)

Illus. 7-23. Use this setup when you make lap joints with the router. The boards on either side are necessary to support the router base during the cut.

Cross-lap and T-shaped lap joints are made in a similar fashion, but you need two guide boards for the two shoulders.

If you will be making a lot of joints on the same size boards, you can make a simple jig to speed up the setup. (See Illus. 7-24.) The two side pieces of the jig should be the same thickness as the board that will be cut. Attach the stops to the

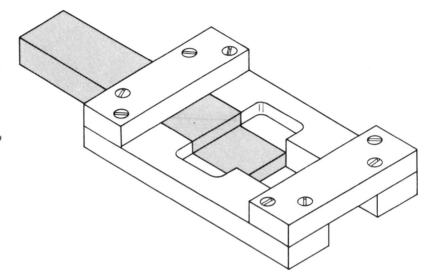

Illus. 7-24. This jig can be used to make half-lap joints with the router. The size of the jig will depend on the size of the board and the diameter of the router base.

side pieces with glue and screws or nails. Make sure that the stops are square with the sides. Make a trial cut on scrap, and cut into the sides of the jig slightly.

To use the jig, place it over the work and line up the cuts in the sides with the layout lines on the work. Then clamp the jig to the bench. Place the router on the jig, and position the bit in the cutout area in the side of the jig. Make sure that the bit will not hit any wood when you start the router. Start the router and make the cuts.

Dadoed-Edge Half-Lap Joint

Edge half-lap joints in solid wood can be weak if the edges are left unsupported. The edge on a dadoed-edge half-lap joint is supported, to prevent breakage along the grain. (See Illus. 7-25.)

To make this joint, install a dado blade on the table saw, and set the blade's width to the thickness of the board. Let's assume that you are using ¾-inch-thick lumber. In such a case, raise the blade height to ⅛ inch. Then make a ¾-inch-wide dado on both sides of the first board. The dadoes have to line up with each other. A stop clamped to the fence can be used to position the work on the mitre gauge. Reset the dado blade to ½ inch and cut two dadoes on the second board.

Now, cut ½-inch-wide notches halfway through both boards. If the boards aren't too wide, use a dado blade. For wider boards, you

Illus. 7-25. The dadoed-edge half-lap joint.

may have to switch to a standard blade or make the cut with a handsaw. (See Illus. 7-26.) Cutting notches in the board with ½-inch-wide dadoes will remove all of the wood between the dado shoulders in the notched area. There will be small shoulders left in the notched area on the board with the ¾-inch-wide dadoes.

Unsupported Lap Joint for Plywood

Long, unsupported lap joints can be used when two parts must cross at a right angle. (See Illus. 7-27.) Although this type of joint is usually weak when used with solid lumber, it can be used with plywood, because the alternating plies eliminate the weakness along the grain that causes problems when the joint is used with solid lumber. This joint is often used to make knockdown furniture. Knockdown furniture is made to be easily assembled and disassembled so that it can be shipped flat and assembled on site.

Lay out the lap joint with a square and then cut the waste out with a sabre saw. Start in from the edge and make one of the long, straight cuts. Cut all the way to the corner; then back up about ¾ inch and make a curving cut to the next corner.

Next, turn off the saw and remove it from the kerf. Make the second straight cut all the way to the corner. (See Illus. 7-28.) The large piece of

waste will fall out. Clean up the end of the cut with the saw. Repeat the procedure for the cut in the mating board; then slide the joint together. As mentioned earlier, this joint is usually used for knockdown items that will be assembled and disassembled repeatedly, so no glue is used in the joint.

Illus. 7-27. Unsupported-edge lap joints can be used with plywood.

Illus. 7-26. After you have cut the dadoes on both parts, make a notch halfway through the dadoed area.

Illus. 7-28. Cut the notch with a sabre saw, also referred to as a jig saw. Make the first cut all the way into the corner; then back up and make a curving cut into the opposite corner. After you make the second long cut, most of the waste will fall out. Cut out the small curved section of waste to complete the notch.

Chapter 8

MITRE JOINTS

The mitre joint can be used for frame, case, and edge joints. (See Illus. 8-1–8-3.) The mitre is a weak joint unless it is reinforced or combined with another type of joint. It is usually only used when appearance is important. The mitre joint hides the end grain of both boards. It can be reinforced with nails, screws, splines, or dowels.

Most mitres are cut to 45 degrees, but you can use any angle for special applications. Mitres can join boards at odd angles, and they can be used to make regular polygons such as hexagons and octagons. (A polygon is a closed figure consisting of straight lines joined end to end. A hexagon is a polygon with six angles and sides. An octagon is a polygon with eight angles and sides.)

When to Use a Mitre

Mitres are often used in projects where they will be highly visible. They are used commonly on picture frames. Mitres are used extensively in finish carpentry. Interior trim is usually mitred. A few examples of places where you would usually use a mitre joint in finish carpentry are: mouldings around windows and doors, base moulding around the floor, and cornice mould-

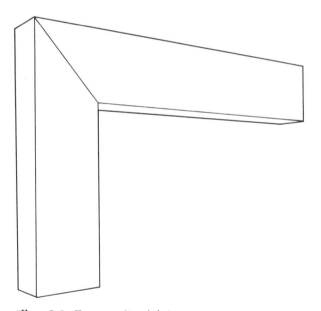

Illus. 8-1. Frame mitre joint.

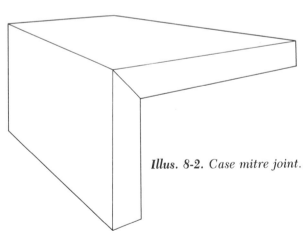

Illus. 8-2. Case mitre joint.

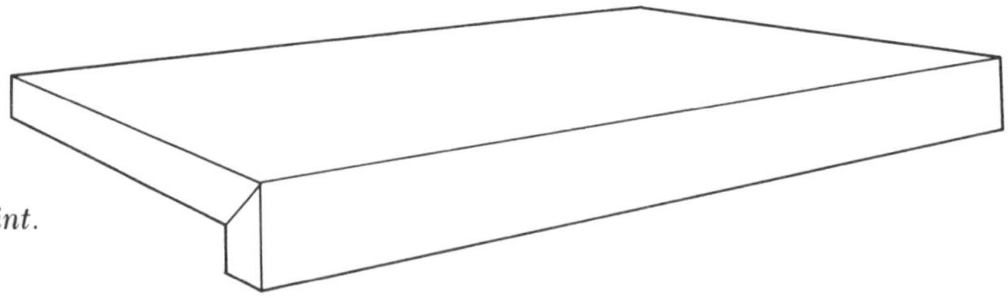

Illus. 8-3. Edge mitre joint.

ing. Mitres can be used to make cabinets, when you don't want any end grain to show. They are most commonly used to join the sides of a cabinet to the top. A splined mitre works well in this instance. (See Illus. 8-4.)

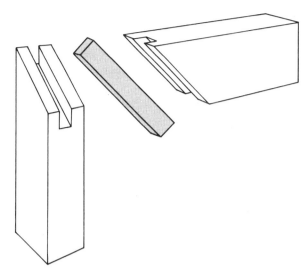

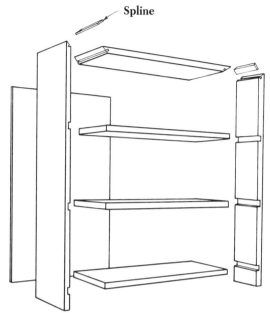

Illus. 8-4. This exploded view of a cabinet shows how splined case mitres can be used to join the side of a cabinet to the top.

Mitre Variations

Because the basic mitre joint is weak, there are many variations in which it is combined with other joints or reinforced. For a full range of mitre variations, consult the *Wood Joiner's Handbook*. Here the easiest and most useful variations are covered.

Splines are one of the best ways to reinforce a mitre joint. For ¾-inch-thick boards, a ⅛-inch-thick spline is usually used. (See Illus. 8-5.)

Dowels can also be used to reinforce a mitre joint. No special jig is needed to make a pegged joint, but you will need a jig specially designed for mitre work to make blind dowel holes in mitred case joints. (See Illus. 8-6.)

Mitre joints can be combined with other stronger joints to increase the strength of the joint

Illus. 8-5. Splines are a good way to reinforce mitre joints. In this illustration, a straight spline is used in a frame mitre.

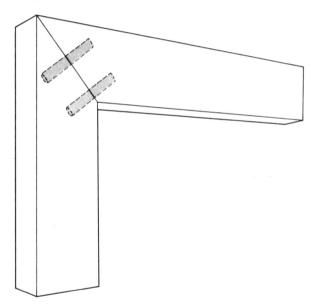

Illus. 8-6. Dowels are often used with mitre joints. In this illustration, blind dowels are used with a frame mitre.

while retaining the appearance of a mitre. The *mitred half-lap joint* is the easiest of these joints to make. It is cut basically the same as a standard half-lap, except that one shoulder is cut on an angle. (See Illus. 8-7.)

Polygons and odd-angled joints can be made using mitres. The only difference in the joint is the mitre angle.

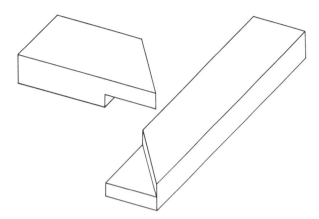

Illus. 8-7. A mitred half-lap joint combines the strength of a half-lap with the look of a mitre.

Compound mitres are joints that angle in two directions. A box with sloping sides, for example, has compound mitres. Compound mitres are often used for picture frames and for mouldings applied to the interior and exterior of homes.

The *coped joint* isn't really a mitre joint, but it looks like one when it is assembled. The coped joint is used primarily when moulding must be joined at an inside corner. It will accommodate walls that are out of square, and will stay tight even if there is a small shift in the walls as the building settles.

Making Mitre Joints

There are many specialized tools for making mitre joints. The simplest is a wood mitre box. It is an open-ended box with slots cut at 90 and 45 degrees. (See Illus. 8-8.) The slots are used to guide the backsaw blade. More sophisticated mitre boxes are made from metal and have adjustable angle guides. A power mitre box combines a circular saw with an adjustable mitre guide. The radial arm saw can be adjusted to cut mitres, and the table saw has a mitre gauge to cut frame mitres, and a blade tilt to cut case and edge mitres.

The most important factor in making mitres is accuracy when cutting the angle. Whether you are using a backsaw and a mitre box or a power tool, make sure that the mitre angle is accurate. A small error in the angle will result in a noticeable gap in the joint. Make test cuts on scrap and place them against a square to test the fit.

Frame Mitres

Using a Mitre Box and Backsaw   Frame mitres are used on picture frames. All you need is a mitre box and backsaw to cut the joint. Make the first cut near the end of the picture-frame mould-

Illus. 8-8. A simple wood mitre box can be used with a backsaw to make many types of mitre joints. You can buy a commercial type or build your own. You can vary the size of a shop-made mitre box to suit your needs. A mitre box 6 inches wide × 3 inches tall × 15 inches long will do most jobs. The front should overhang the bottom by ¼ inch. Let the lip catch on the front of the bench to help steady the mitre box. Lay out the slots with an accurate square. Cut the slots after the box has been assembled.

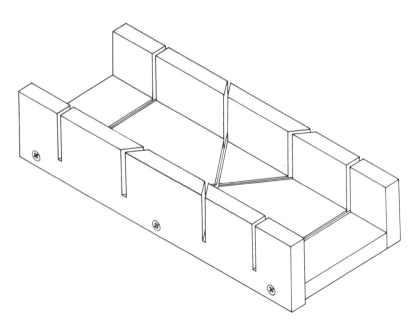

ing. Place the moulding in the mitre box face up, with its outside edge against the back of the box. Saw straight down across the face of the moulding. (See Illus. 8-9.)

Illus. 8-9. Using a mitre box to cut a piece of picture-frame moulding.

Picture-frame moulding has a rabbet in its edge for the picture and glass to fit into. The important dimension of a picture frame is the inside measurement of the rabbet. After you have cut one end of the moulding, place a square on the back of the moulding and line up the square's blade with the point where the rabbet intersects the mitre cut. Draw a line that extends to the edge of the moulding.

Now, measure the distance from the outside end of the mitre to the line. Double this dimension and add it to the size of the picture to get the outside dimensions of the frame. If you will be installing glass, add another ⅛ inch. Glass will expand and contract with changes in temperature, so you must leave some room for expansion or the glass may crack.

Now, mark the length of the first side of the frame on the moulding. Place the moulding in the mitre box and put the saw in the slot. Line up the mark with the edge of the saw. Make sure that the saw kerf will be on the waste side of the line, and then saw through the moulding.

Before measuring the next part, you have to cut a new mitre on the end of the moulding. The cut left on the end after the previous cut will be the opposite angle from what is needed. Place the moulding in the mitre box and make the new

cut as close to the end as possible. Now, measure the next side and cut it.

Use the previously cut part to mark the opposite side. It is important that the opposite sides are exactly the same length. If they aren't, the joints won't fit well. Repeat the above procedure to cut the other two sides.

Now, assemble the joint. A mitre clamp makes this easier. Place two mating parts in the clamp and adjust their position until the joint lines up. After you have adjusted their position, clamp one part firmly in place and remove the other part to apply glue to its ends. Apply a thin coat to both ends. Do not use too much glue, to minimize the amount of squeeze-out on the face of the moulding.

Replace the part in the clamp. Drill a small pilot hole for a nail. (See Illus. 8-10.) Drive a small finish nail into the joint. Set the head slightly. Don't set it too deep, because there isn't a lot of wood for the head to grab.

Illus. 8-10. A mitre clamp is useful for holding the parts in alignment as you drill the pilot holes and drive the nails into the joint.

Assemble the rest of the joints in the same way. When you get to the last side, you will need to apply glue to both ends at one time.

After assembly, place the glass and the picture in the frame. Put a piece of cardboard behind the picture. Use glazing points to hold the picture in place.

Glazing points are small metal fasteners that are used to hold glass in place. You can get a special gun that "shoots" diamond-shaped glazing points. You don't need a special gun to install the type that has a point on one end and bent tabs on the other. Lay the glazing point flat against the cardboard and press the point against the wood of the frame. Place a screwdriver blade against the tabs on the glazing point and push the point into the wood.

Using a Table Saw   A frame mitre can be made on the table saw if you use the mitre gauge as a

Illus. 8-12. To cut a frame mitre with the table saw, set the mitre gauge to 45 degrees. A wood extension attached to the fence is helpful for supporting the cut; you can clamp a stop to the extension when making multiple cuts of the same length.

the fence to gauge the length of the part. (See Illus. 8-12.)

The joint can be assembled using glue and nails or screws. Dowels and splines can also be used. Directions for making dowel joints and splined mitres are given later in this chapter.

Edge Mitres

An edge mitre is usually a long joint. (See Illus. 8-13.) The table saw is one of the best ways to make this joint. Set the tilt arbor to 45 degrees. Position the fence so that the saw teeth face away from the fence. Measure the distance required between the blade and the fence, and lock the fence in place.

Place the edge of the board against the fence and feed the board through the saw. (See Illus. 8-14.) Don't stand in the blade's path, because there is a possibility that the waste may kick back at the end of the cut. Note from Illus. 8-14 that with the fence in this position, the "good" side of the cut is above the blade, and the waste side is below the blade. This is the best way to make the cut, because if the board lifts from the table slightly, you can simply make another pass to correct the joint. If the fence is placed on the

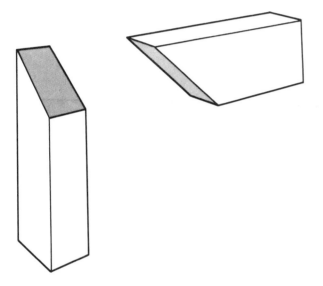

Illus. 8-11. An exploded view of the frame mitre.

guide. (See Illus. 8-11.) With the mitre gauge set to 90 degrees, precut the parts to rough length. Leave them slightly longer than needed. Then set the mitre gauge to 45 degrees. A wood extension on the fence will help to support the work as you make the cuts.

Make a mitre cut on the end of each part. Place the outside edge of the board against the mitre gauge, with the board front face up. Move the mitre gauge to the opposite slot and reset it to the opposite 45-degree setting. Cut a piece of scrap with this new setting, and check the fit of the joint. Use a square to make sure that the joint is 90 degrees. If necessary, readjust the mitre gauge and try again.

Now, cut the second mitre on each board. A stop can be clamped to a wood extension on

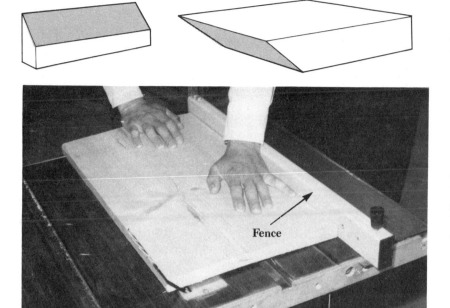

Illus. 8-13. Exploded view of an edge mitre.

Illus. 8-14. The edge mitre is cut with the blade tilted to 45 degrees. Place the fence so that the "good" side of the cut will be above the blade.

other side of the blade, then the "good" part of the joint will be below the blade. In this case, if the board were to lift up from the table during the cut, the joint would be ruined.

Cut the mating part using the same technique, and then make a trial assembly. Secure the joint with glue and nails, or use a spline as described later in this section.

Case Mitres

Case mitres join the end of one board to the end of the mating board. (See Illus. 8-15.) Case mitres can be made in a mitre box, if the boards are narrow. Place the board on its edge in the mitre box with its face against the back of the box, and then cut a mitre on one end of the board. Measure from the cut end to mark the length of the part. Make the cut on the opposite end, lining up the length mark with the saw blade. Make sure that the entire saw kerf will be on the waste side of the line. Cut the rest of the parts and assemble the joint.

There are two ways to make case mitres on the table saw. If the boards are narrow, use the mitre gauge; for wider boards, use the fence. In both cases, you need to set the tilt arbor to 45 degrees.

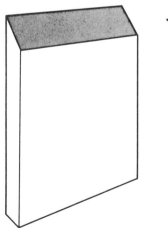

Illus. 8-15. An exploded view of a case mitre.

To make a case mitre on a narrow board, begin by setting the mitre gauge to 90 degrees. Place the board on the saw, with the board's inside face against the table and its edge against the mitre gauge. Note that the blade tilts away from the mitre gauge. (See Illus. 8-16.) Make all of the cuts using this same setup.

Illus. 8-16. To make a case mitre on a narrow board, set the blade tilt to 45 degrees and guide the cut with the mitre gauge.

To make a case mitre on the end of a wide board, a special setup using the saw fence has to be used. This method is particularly useful when working with plywood or particleboard, because you are more likely to have wide pieces that are mitred. Be careful when you use this technique. The waste piece will be between the saw blade and the fence. This can lead to a kickback. Don't stand in the blade's path as you make the cut. The method of attaching a wood fence described here will help to minimize kickback, but kickback is still possible, so take precautions. *Note:* All the parts that will be mitred using this method must be cut to exact size before you cut the mitres.

Start by clamping a piece of wood to the fence. Raise this wood auxiliary fence off the table. There should be a gap that is equal to the thickness of the board minus ⅛ inch. With the board against the fence, the top ⅛ inch of the board should be in contact with the auxiliary wood fence. Position the fence so that the distance between the blade and the face of the wood fence is equal to the thickness of the board to be cut. (See Illus. 8-17.)

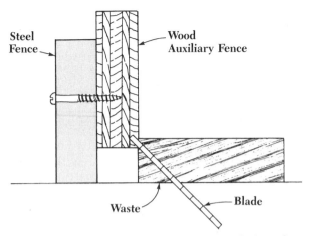

Illus. 8-17. To make a case mitre on a wide board, you first have to attach a wooden auxiliary fence to the steel fence. Raise the auxiliary fence off the table to leave a space for the waste from the cut. This will help to minimize the possibility of a kickback.

Set the blade tilt to 45 degrees and then lower the blade. Then turn on the saw and slowly raise the blade until its teeth just begin to cut into the wood fence. (See Illus. 8-18.) Then turn off the saw.

Illus. 8-18. Set the blade tilt to 45 degrees and lower the blade. Then move the fence into position. Start the saw and raise the blade until it just barely cuts into the wooden auxiliary fence.

Now, test the setup. Make a cut on the end of a scrap and check the accuracy of the setup. Make any adjustment necessary. You will need to lower the blade before you change the saw angle, and then raise it with the saw running, to cut into the wood fence. When you are satisfied with the way the test joint fits, make the cuts on the project boards. (See Illus. 8-19.)

Illus. 8-19. Using the raised wood auxiliary fence allows you to cut a case mitre on large parts such as this piece of siding.

Splined Mitres

Splines are a very good way to reinforce mitres. (See Illus. 8-20.) The groove is usually made on the table saw. A ⅛-inch hardboard spline can be used. The spline will reinforce the joint, and it makes it easier to assemble, because it holds the parts in proper alignment during clamping.

The procedure for making edge and case mitres with splines is the same. Cut the mitres using one of the methods described above. Then set the blade tilt on the saw to 45 degrees and position the fence as shown in Illus. 8-21, with the blade tilting away from the fence. Make a test cut on a scrap that has been cut to 45 degrees.

Use the mitre gauge to guide the cut when the boards are narrow. With wider boards, it is not necessary to use the mitre gauge; the fence will guide the work. Adjust the fence position and the blade height until you get a groove that is about ⅛ inch up from the inside edge of the joint and about half as deep as the distance between the face of the joint and the face of the board. Now, cut the groove in all of the joints.

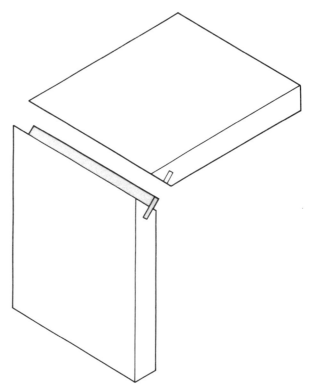

Illus. 8-20. An exploded view of a splined case mitre joint.

Illus. 8-21. To cut a spline groove in a case mitre, set the blade tilt to 45 degrees. Place the fence so that the blade angles away from it. Raise the blade to make a groove about halfway through the board. The groove should be placed about ⅛ inch away from the inside edge of the joint.

Test-assemble one joint and measure the width needed for the spline. Cut the spline from ⅛-inch-thick hardboard. Sand the edges to remove the fuzz left by the saw. Apply glue to the joint and spread glue in the spline groove.

Insert the spline into one side of the joint. Assemble the joint, lining up the spline with the groove in the mating board. (See Illus. 8-22.) Clamp the joint with bar clamps and let the glue set.

Illus. 8-22. Assembling a splined case mitre joint.

Plate splines (biscuits) can also be used to reinforce a mitre joint. To use them for edge and case mitres, you will need a plate-joining machine that has an adjustable fence or an auxiliary mitre fence. (See Illus. 8-23.)

Illus. 8-23. A plate joiner can be used to add a plate spline that will reinforce a case mitre. A 45-degree mitre fence is used for the operation.

Cut the mitres first. Then place the parts next to each other and mark the spline locations. For maximum strength, place the splines so that there will be about ½ inch between them. Set up the machine to make a 45-degree cut. Refer to the owner's manual for complete details.

Place the board with its inside face up on the bench. With some machines, the mitre base of the plate joiner is placed on the bench. With others, the mitre fence is placed on the face of the board. Refer to the owner's manual for complete directions. Line up the index mark on the base with the line on the joint. Make the cut. Then repeat the procedure for the rest of the plate locations.

Apply glue to the joint and spread it inside all of the spline pockets. Insert the plates into one side of the joint. Assemble the joint and clamp it.

There are two types of splines that can be used with frame mitres: the straight spline and the feather spline. (See Illus. 8-24.) A tenoning jig is needed to make either joint on the table saw.

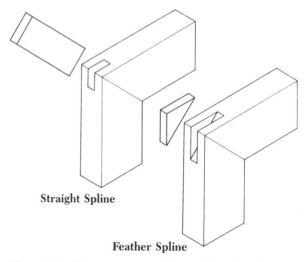

Straight Spline

Feather Spline

Illus. 8-24. Face mitres can be reinforced with a straight or a feather spline.

To make a straight spline joint, first cut the mitres. Then set up the tenoning jig as shown in Illus. 8-25. Set the guide on the jig to 45 degrees, and position the clamp to hold the board.

Next, mark the outside face on all of the boards. Insert the board into the jig with the

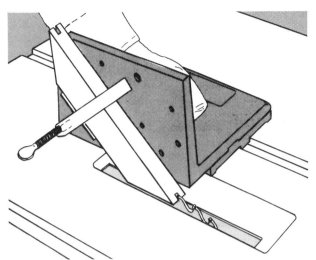

Illus. **8-25.** *Using a tenoning jig to cut a spline groove in a frame mitre.*

Illus. **8-26.** *Assembling a splined-face mitre. The ends of the spline will be trimmed after the joint is assembled.*

board's outside face against the jig. Let the mitre cut rest flat against the saw table. Tighten the clamp and make sure that the edge is against the guide.

Adjust the position of the tenoning jig to center the cut. Raise the blade about ½ inch above the table. You can make the cut deeper, if you want to use a wider spline to give the joint additional strength.

Use this setup to cut all of the joints on one end of the boards. If the cut is centered exactly, turn the boards around and make the rest of the cuts with the boards' inside faces against the jig. Since it is difficult to center the cut exactly, it is better to make all of the cuts with the same face against the jig; this way, any inaccuracy will be compensated for, and the face of the joint will be flush. To do this, you will need to reposition the guide and clamp on the jig so that the board is facing the opposite direction.

Now, cut a spline from ⅛-inch-thick hardboard. If you made the groove ½ inch deep, the spline should be 1 inch wide. Make the spline longer than needed so that you can trim it to fit. Apply glue to the groove and the rest of the joint and insert the spline. (See Illus. 8-26.)

Assemble the joint and clamp it. After the glue is dry, trim off the ends of the spline so that they are flush with the edges of the boards. Use a backsaw to cut off the excess spline, and then sand the ends flush with the boards.

The feather spline is faster to make, because the groove is cut in both mating boards at the same time. This joint is more visible than the straight spline. It is often used for decorative effect, in which case a piece of hardwood instead of hardboard can be used. If you use the dado blade to make the cut, the spline can be made thicker so that it will be more visible.

Set up the tenoning jig as shown in Illus. 8-27. Two guides are used. Both are set to 45 degrees, but in opposite directions. Two clamps hold the parts.

Insert two mating parts into the jig and adjust them so that the joint is tight. Clamp them in place with the clamps on the jig. Raise the blade to make a cut as deep as possible without hitting the guides on the tenoning jig. Adjust the tenoning jig to center the cut. After making the cut on the first joint, reposition the board to make the cut on the next joint.

Cut the spline oversize. The spline can be cut rectangular at this stage; it will be trimmed to a triangular shape after assembly. Apply glue to the joint and assemble it. After the mating boards are together, slip the spline into the groove. (See Illus. 8-28.)

The plate joiner can also be used to reinforce frame mitres. In this case, you don't need a mitre fence on the tool. The joint is cut into the mitred end of the parts. Place the fence on the face of the board and press the front edge of the base

Illus. 8-27. With the tenoning jig set up like this, you can cut the groove for a feather spline. The groove is cut in both mating boards in a single operation.

Illus. 8-28. Assemble the joint first, and then slip the feather spline into the groove. The spline is trimmed flush after the glue dries.

Illus. 8-29. A plate joiner can be used to reinforce frame mitres. The pocket is cut in the mitred end of the joint.

against the mitred end. Turn on the tool and cut a pocket into the end. (See Illus. 8-29.) After you have cut the pockets on all of the parts, apply glue to the joint and inside the pockets. Insert a plate spline into the pocket and assemble the joint.

Dowelled Mitres

Mitre joints can be reinforced with dowels. The simplest dowel to use is the pegged dowel. The pegged dowel can be used for frame, case, and edge mitres. (See Illus. 8-30.) To make the joint,

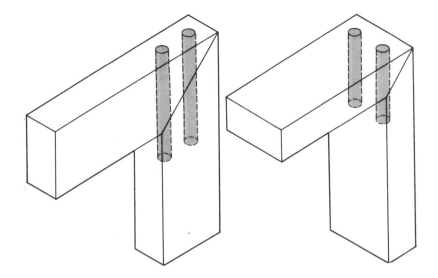

Illus. 8-30. Mitre joints can be reinforced with pegged dowels.

cut a standard mitre as described above, and then place the parts together as you drill the holes. If you want, glue and assemble the parts first, and then drill the dowel holes after the glue is dry. It makes it easier to keep the parts in alignment as you drill the holes. Drill the holes deep enough so that the dowel will penetrate about ¾ inch or more into the second board. Spread glue around the inside of the dowel hole and drive the dowels into the holes. Trim the ends with a backsaw, and then sand them flush.

When you don't want the ends of the dowels to show, make a blind dowel joint. In a blind joint, the dowel holes must be drilled at a 90-degree angle to the mitred end of the board. This is not difficult to do with frame joints because most dowelling jigs can be used to do the job. Edge and case joints, however, require a special type of jig. It is usually better to use a spline joint for edge and case mitres.

To add blind dowels to a frame mitre, cut the mitre using one of the methods described earlier. Place the parts side by side and use a square to make the dowel locations on both boards. Two dowels are usually all that are needed, unless the joint is very wide.

Clamp one board in the vise at a 45-degree angle. Place the dowel jig on the end of the board and line up the index mark with the layout line. Set a depth stop on the drill bit, or wrap a piece of tape around the bit to indicate when to stop

drilling. (See Illus. 8-31.) Drill the hole, and then reposition the jig for the other hole on this end.

Repeat the procedure for the mating board. Make sure that the jig fence is against the same face of the board each time you reposition it.

Apply glue to the joint and spread glue around the inside of the dowel holes. Insert the dowels into the holes in one side of the joint. Assemble the joint and clamp it.

Illus. 8-31. Blind dowel holes can be made in frame mitres with a dowelling jig. Position the jig so that the base is flat against the mitred end of the board.

Mitred Half-Lap Joints

A mitred half-lap joint is much stronger than an ordinary frame mitre. (See Illus. 8-32.) This joint is not much harder to make than an ordinary half-lap.

Illus. 8-32. The mitred half-lap joint is a strong variation of the frame mitre.

A separate setup is required for each of the two parts of the joint. In these directions, one part will be referred to as A, and the other part B. (See Illus. 8-33.) Begin by cutting a standard half-lap on the end of part A. (See Chapter 7.) Then set the mitre gauge to 45 degrees and cut off the end of the part. (See Illus. 8-34.)

Now, set up the tenoning jig to make the cheek cut on part B. Attach a guide to the jig at a 45-degree angle and install one of the clamps. Insert part B into the jig and let its corner rest against the saw table. Make sure that its edge is against the guide and clamp. Adjust the position of the tenoning jig so that all of the saw kerf will be on the waste side. Raise the blade until the cut will reach the corner of the board. Then turn on the saw and make the cut. (See Illus. 8-35.)

Remove part B from the tenoning jig. Lower the blade to make the shoulder cut. Set the mitre gauge to 45 degrees. Place part B against the mitre gauge. Line up the board with the blade so that the shoulder will begin exactly at the corner of the board. Turn on the saw and make the shoulder cut.

The joint is now ready for assembly. Apply glue to the joint surfaces and put the joint together. Clamp across the joint until the glue dries.

Making Polygons

A polygon is any multi-sided shape. Most of the time, you will want to make a regular polygon that has sides that are all equal in length. Face mitres for regular polygons can be cut on the table saw with the mitre gauge. Edge and case mitres can be made by adjusting the blade tilt.

You need to know the correct angle to set the mitre gauge or blade tilt. The chart shown in Table 8-1 gives the mitre angle for several common polygons. Note that there are two angles listed. The *mitre angle* is used when you are setting the blade tilt for case joints. The *mitre gauge angle* is used to set the mitre gauge for frame

Illus. 8-33. The steps necessary to cut a mitred half-lap joint with the tenoning jig.

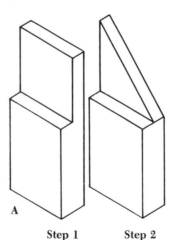

A

Step 1   Step 2

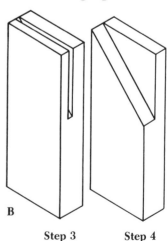

B

Step 3   Step 4

Illus. 8-34. After cutting a standard half-lap on part A, cut the end to 45 degrees.

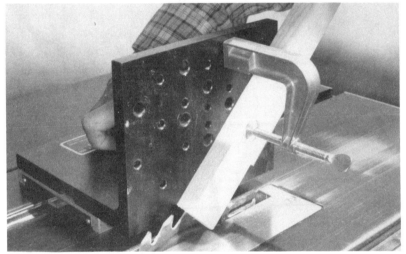

Illus. 8-35. With a guide set to 45 degrees, use the tenoning jig to make the cheek cut on part B.

joints. The difference is in the way the scales are usually made. The blade-tilt gauge starts at 0 degrees, indicating a square cut, while the mitre gauge uses 90 degrees to indicate a square cut.

Mitre Angles for Regular Polygons

No. of Sides	Mitre Angle	Mitre Gauge
3	60	30
4	45	45
5	36	54
6	30	60
7	25.7	64.3
8	22.5	67.5
12	15	75
15	12	78
20	9	81

Table 8-1. Mitre angles for regular polygons.

Face mitres are used to make projects that are flat, such as a picture frame. To make a face mitre, find the mitre-gauge angle on the chart and set the mitre gauge. For an octagon (eight-sided piece), the angle is 67.5 degrees. Since a small error will be multiplied by the number of joints, accuracy is essential. Test the setup by cutting a set of parts from scrap and assembling them. Make adjustments as necessary to get a tight-fitting joint.

There are two ways you can cut the joints. The easier method can be used with flat boards. If you are using moulding, you will need to use the second method, which requires two setups.

First Method For the first method, use the same mitre-gauge setup to cut both ends. Begin by cutting the angle on one end of the board. (See Illus. 8-36.)

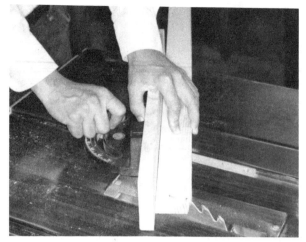

Illus. 8-36. Making the first cut for the octagon.

Now, flip the board over and cut the part to length. You can add a wood fence to the mitre gauge and clamp a stop to the fence to cut the parts to length. Butt the end of the board against the stop. The angle that is left on the board can be used for the next part, so flip the board over again and cut the next part to length. Continue in this manner until you have all of the parts cut. (See Illus. 8-37.)

Illus. 8-37. To make sure that all of the pieces are the same length, clamp a stop to a wood extension on the mitre gauge.

Second Method If you are using moulding, you have to use the second method. With this method, it is best to cut the parts to rough length with the mitre gauge set to 90 degrees. Leave them a little long.

Now, set the mitre gauge to the correct angle and cut one end on all of the parts. To cut the other ends, reset the mitre gauge to the same angle, but on the opposite side of 90 degrees. Move the mitre gauge to the slot on the opposite side of the blade. Next, cut the parts to length using this setup.

Once you have cut the parts using either method, you are ready to assemble them. Apply glue to the ends and lay the parts flat on the bench. Lay the parts on a piece of wax paper. The wax paper will keep the glue from sticking to the bench. A web clamp is the best clamp to use on the joints. Adjust the diameter of its loop to fit around the work. Place the loop around the edge, and then tighten it with a wrench. (See Illus. 8-38.) Let the glue set before removing the clamp.

If the project is purely for decorative purposes, you can sometimes just glue the joint. For added strength, drill pilot holes and drive nails or screws into the joint after the glue is set, or use splines or dowels to reinforce the joint.

An edge joint can also be used to make a polygon. This joint is used to make projects that are long instead of flat, such as an octagonal pedestal or a box with an arched top. Even though the arched top is not a complete polygon, the procedure for cutting the joints is the same. (See Illus. 8-39.)

The first step in making the edge joint is to find the correct angle on the chart and set the blade tilt. The angle for an octagon is 22.5 degrees.

Set the fence to the width of the parts. Rip the parts from a wider board. Place the fence on the side opposite the direction of the tilt. This will put the waste on the underside of the cut. Now, turn the parts around, and, using the same saw setup, cut the angle on the other side of the parts. (See Illus. 8-40.)

Illus. 8-38. *A web clamp is a loop of strong cloth webbing that can be tightened with a ratchet assembly. The web clamp is a very good way to clamp many-sided projects such as this octagon-shaped picture frame.*

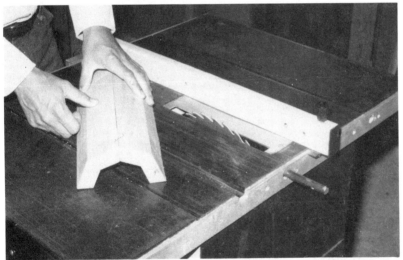

Illus. 8-39. *By adjusting the blade tilt to the angles listed in the chart on page 83, you can make edge joints such as this. The parts shown here will be used to make an arched top for a small box.*

Illus. 8-40. *When making odd-angle mitres, set the blade tilt to the angle listed in the chart on page 81. Position the fence so that the blade is tilted away from it.*

Compound-Angle Mitres

When boards that are placed on a slope meet at a corner, you can't simply cut the ends to 45 degrees to make a mitre cut. The joint must angle in two directions. This is called a compound angle. A box with sloping sides is an example of a project that would use compound-angle mitres. (See Illus. 8-41.)

Compound angles can be cut in two ways. Narrow boards are usually made with the first method. This method is used on projects such as a picture frame. The second method is used when the boards are wider.

The first method is fairly simple. When you cut the mitre, place the board in the mitre box on the angle that it will be in the finished project. Then cut the joint as usual. The compound angle is formed automatically as you cut.

When using the second method, you have to know the angles you will be using, because both the blade and the mitre gauge must be set to an angle. This is the method you would use to make a box or other large object with sloping sides. First, determine the angle of the side slope. (See Illus. 8-42.) You can determine the angle by setting a sliding T bevel to the desired angle, and then placing the bevel against a protractor, with the handle against the bottom, and reading the angle where the blade crosses the scale.

Most protractors are set up with 90 degrees in the center of the scale. You need to know the number of degrees off of 90 degrees, so subtract the scale reading from 90; this will give you the side slope. Table 8-2 lists the angles for a square, hexagon, and octagon. If you need to use other angles, refer to the *Wood Joiner's Handbook* for instructions on how to determine the angles.

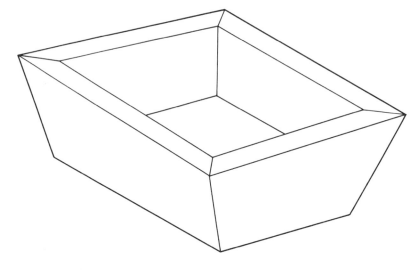

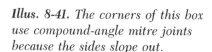

Illus. 8-41. The corners of this box use compound-angle mitre joints because the sides slope out.

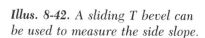

Illus. 8-42. A sliding T bevel can be used to measure the side slope.

Compound Mitre Angles

Square

Side Slope	5°	10°	15°	20°	30°
Mitre Gauge	85°	80.25°	75.5°	71.25°	63.5°
Blade Tilt	44.75°	44.25°	43.25°	41.75°	37.75°

Hexagon (six sides)

Side Slope	5°	10°	15°	20°	30°
Mitre Gauge	87.5°	84.5°	81.75°	79°	74°
Blade Tilt	29.75°	29.5°	29°	28.25°	26°

Octagon (eight sides)

Side Slope	5°	10°	15°	20°	30°
Mitre Gauge	88°	86°	84°	82°	78.25°
Blade Tilt	22.25°	22°	21.5°	21°	19.5°

Table 8-2. Compound mitre angles.

To make the cuts on the table saw, use the mitre gauge in combination with the blade tilt. You can also use the radial arm saw or a power mitre box. In some cases, you may need to convert the angle to a different type of scale when you use another type of saw. The mitre-gauge angle in the chart can be used for any scale that uses 90 degrees to indicate a square cut. If the scale on your saw uses 0 degrees to indicate a square cut, then convert the listed angle by subtracting it from 90.

The blade-tilt angle is listed for a scale that uses 0 degrees to indicate a square cut. If the scale on your saw uses 90 degrees to indicate a square cut, convert the angle by subtracting it from 90.

Cut the parts to rough length with the blade and mitre gauge set to make a square cut. Then find the correct angles on the chart. Set the mitre gauge and the blade tilt to the angles listed. For example, let's assume that a box with sides that slope 15 degrees is being made. The mitre gauge angle is 75.5 degrees, and the blade tilt is 43.25 degrees. Cut one end of each part using this setup.

Now, reset the mitre gauge to the same angle, but on the opposite side of 90 degrees. Make the second cut on each board using this setup. (See Illus. 8-43.)

To assemble, clamp one part in a vise and apply glue to the joint. Hold the mating part in place and drill pilot holes. Then drive nails into the joint. Repeat this step for the rest of the joints.

Illus. 8-43. Cutting a compound-angle mitre joint.

Using Mitres in Finish Carpentry

The mitre joint is probably the most frequently used joint in finish carpentry. Mitre joints are used for door casing, window trim, baseboards, and ceiling mouldings.

Door casing and window trim usually use a standard frame mitre. The moulding should be placed ¼ inch away from the edge of the opening. This serves two purposes. First, it leaves clearance for hinges, and second, it makes the installation look better. If you place a moulding flush with the opening, any irregularities will be obvious; but, if the moulding is set back ¼ inch, minor irregularities in the opening or the edge of the moulding won't show.

The moulding can be cut with a handsaw in a mitre box or with power equipment. Cut the mitre on the vertical parts first. Install them with a couple of nails, but don't drive the heads all the way in, in case you need to make some adjustments later.

Next, measure the length of the head casing. Cut the mitres on the head casing and test the fit. (See Illus. 8-44.) If the joints fit well, apply glue to the joints and then nail the head casing in place.

Illus. 8-44. The head casing is applied last. Note that the moulding is set back from the edge ¼ inch.

Use 4d or 6d casing nails along the inside edge of the moulding, and 8d casing nails along the outside edge. Space the nails about 16 inches apart. Drive one 6d nail down from the top edge of the moulding through the joint to lock the joint together. If the moulding splits when you drive the nails, drill pilot holes for the nails to prevent the splitting. Set the nails below the surface of the moulding with a nail set, and then fill the holes with wood putty.

Baseboard and other types of mouldings require a case mitre. You can make this joint with a backsaw and a mitre box, if the moulding will fit in the box standing on its edge. Place the moulding in the mitre box with its edge against the bottom of the box and its rear face against the back of the box. Put the backsaw in the mitre slot and make the cut. (See Illus. 8-45.)

A coped joint is often used in place of a mitre when moulding meets at an inside corner. Baseboard and quarter-round and cove mouldings are examples of mouldings that can be coped. (See Illus. 8-46.)

Illus. 8-45. When the moulding is small enough to fit on edge in the mitre box, you can cut case mitres like this.

Illus. 8-46. The coped joint is often used instead of a mitre on inside corners. The coped joint works better when the corner is out of square, and it won't open up as the building settles.

Cut the end of the first piece square, and long enough to fit all the way into the corner. Make a mitre cut on the mating part. (See Illus. 8-47.) Use a coping saw to cut along the profile left by the mitre cut. (See Illus. 8-48.) Place the coped part over the mating part and test the fit. Make fine adjustments with a pocket knife.

Nail the moulding in place. Don't glue the joint. Leaving the joint unglued allows the parts

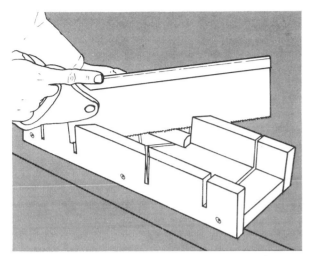

Illus. 8-47. The first step in cutting the coped joint is to cut a mitre on the end of the board.

Illus. 8-48. Use a coping saw to make the cope cut. Follow the profile left by the mitre cut. Make the cut square with the face of the moulding.

to shift as the building settles. The coped joint allows the parts to move and still maintain a tight joint.

Some types of moulding require a compound-angle mitre. Cornice moulding is one example. (Cornice moulding is a horizontal member that is used on top of an architectural composition.) In Illus. 8-49, a piece of cornice moulding is being held against the ceiling next to a wall. Note how the moulding is angled out from the wall. This job is fairly simple because of the way the moulding is made. The moulding has a flat section along its inside edge. To cut the moulding in a

mitre box, place the moulding in the mitre box so that this edge is flat on the bottom of the box. This will put the moulding at an angle in the box.

Rest the other edge against the back of the box. Hold the moulding at the angle and make the mitre cut as usual. The resulting cut will angle in two directions. When you assemble the joint, the moulding will be angled away from the wall at the same angle that it was placed in the mitre box. (See Illus. 8-50.)

Illus. 8-49. When properly applied, this type of cornice moulding sits at an angle. You must make a compound-angle mitre at the corner.

Illus. 8-50. Cornice moulding with a compound-mitre joint.

Chapter 9

MORTISE-AND-TENON JOINTS

The mortise-and-tenon joint is one of the strongest frame joints. The tenon is a projection on the end of one board that fits into a mortise that is cut out on the other board. A mortise can be blind or through. Illus. 9-1 shows a typical mortise-and-tenon joint. Note the terminology used to designate the parts of the joint and its dimensions. These terms will be referred to throughout this chapter.

When to Use a Mortise-and-Tenon Joint

Whenever a great deal of strength is needed, the mortise-and-tenon joint is a good choice. The

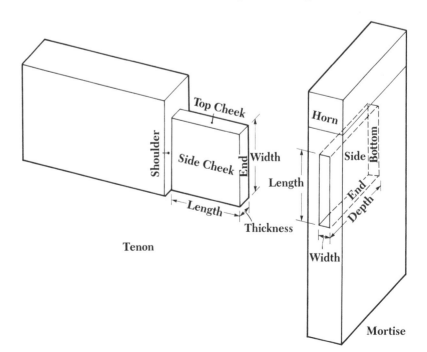

Illus. 9-1. The mortise-and-tenon joint is a frame joint. Note the labels designating the parts and dimensions of the joint.

mortise and tenon is a traditional joint, and therefore, very appropriate when making antique reproductions. When you are set up with the jigs described later in this chapter, you can make a mortise-and-tenon joint almost as quickly as a dowel joint. In most cases, a mortise and tenon will be stronger, so if you have the equipment, use the mortise and tenon for all frame joints that you make.

A mortise-and-tenon joint is the best joint to use for joining the frame members in a frame-and-panel cabinet door. These joints are subjected to a lot of stress, particularly on the hinge side of the door. The mortise-and-tenon joint is well suited to withstand this stress. The panel in the center of the door fits in a groove. If you use the haunched tenon described in the section on joint variations, you can cut the groove all the way to the end of the board, because the tenon will fit in the groove.

Post-and-panel cabinets are made with large frame members that run from the bottom of the cabinet's leg to the top of the cabinet. Smaller rails are attached to these posts with mortise-and-tenon joints. Grooves are cut into the spaces between the posts and rails; the panels are fit into these spaces.

Chairs can be assembled with dowel joints, but for the maximum strength, use mortise-and-tenon joints where the rails and stretchers attach to the legs. The stretchers and rails of a table will also be stronger if you use mortise-and-tenon joints to attach them.

Mortise-and-Tenon Variations

The *through mortise and tenon* is a traditional joint that is often found in antiques. (See Illus. 9-2.) The end of the tenon is visible in this joint. If you are chopping the mortises by hand, lay out the mortise on both edges of the board and chop halfway through from each edge. If you are using a router, either use a long bit or cut in halfway from both edges. For a traditional look, square-up the corners of the router-cut mortise.

Glue is sufficiently strong to hold a well-fitting mortise and tenon without further reinforcement, but when you are making an antique reproduction, you may want to wedge or peg a through mortise and tenon. Wedges and pegs were used in earlier times when glue wasn't as reliable as it is today. The *open mortise* is one of the easiest types to make, because you can cut the entire joint with a table saw.

Most modern furniture uses a *blind mortise*. (See Illus. 9-3.) The blind mortise is almost as strong as a through mortise, and is easier to make with power tools. The joint is completely hidden when assembled. When a router is used to make the mortise, the ends of the mortise are rounded. Round the top and bottom cheeks of the tenon with a file, to match the mortise.

For frame-and-panel construction, a *haunched tenon* is usually used. The stiles and rails of the frame are grooved along the inside edge; the panel will fit into this groove. The mortise is made the same width as the groove. A small projection on the top of the tenon fits into the groove; the rest of the tenon fits into the mortise. This makes a stronger joint and fills the groove on the end of the stile.

The *stub tenon* is very easy to make, but it isn't as strong as a haunched tenon. No mortise is needed, because the stub tenon fits into the groove in the stile. Make the groove deeper than usual to increase the strength of the joint.

The stub tenon is best used when you are using a plywood panel, because the panel can be glued into the frame. The panel will strengthen the door, so some of the stress is taken off the frame joints. If you use a solid-wood panel, you can't glue it in the groove. It must be left free to expand and contract with changes in humidity; otherwise, it will split or push the joints apart. For solid-wood panels, the haunched tenon is better, because the corner joints must take all of the stress applied to the door.

When the mortised board is thicker than the tenoned board, you can use a *barefaced tenon*. (See Illus. 9-4.) The barefaced tenon can take

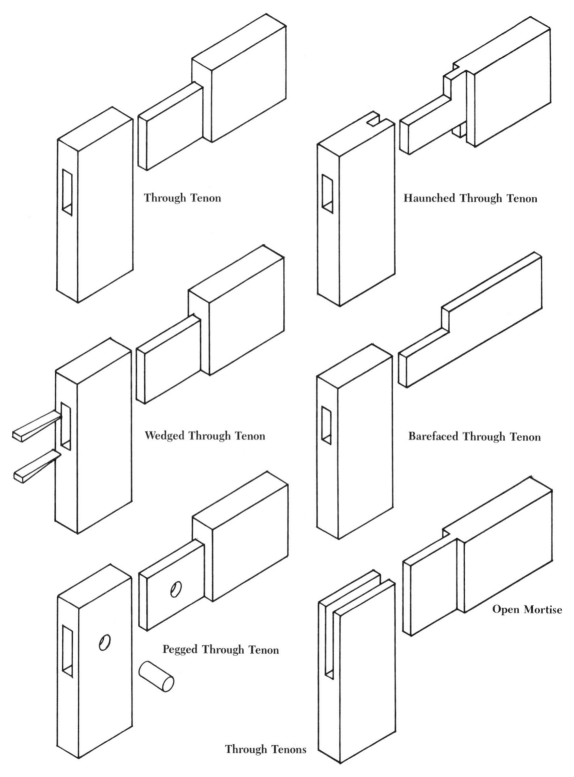

Through Tenon

Haunched Through Tenon

Wedged Through Tenon

Barefaced Through Tenon

Pegged Through Tenon

Open Mortise

Through Tenons

Illus. 9-2. *The end of a tenon in a through mortise-and-tenon joint is visible. The tenon goes all the way through the mortised board. This type of joint is often used on antique reproductions.*

several forms. The simplest type of barefaced tenon fits into a mortise that is the same dimensions as the tenon board. The end of the board fits into the mortise.

Other types of barefaced tenons have one or two shoulders. Using a barefaced tenon makes the joint stronger, because a thicker tenon can be used. You can use a router to cut the mortise if you round the tenon to fit or if you square-up the mortise with a chisel.

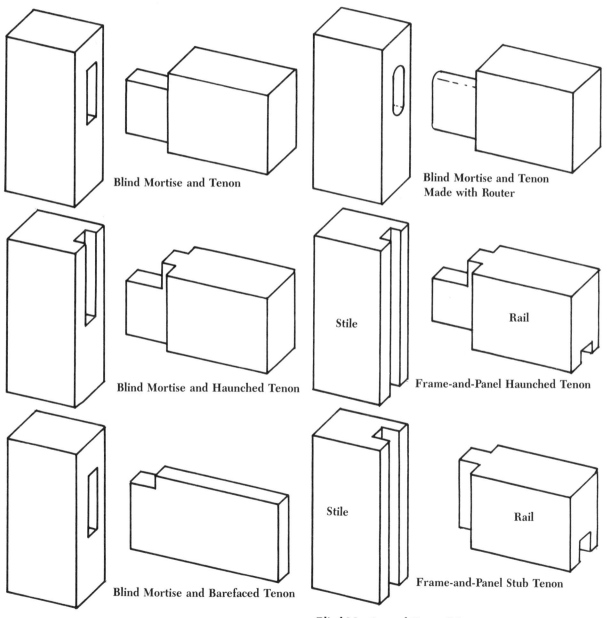

Blind Mortise and Tenon

Blind Mortise and Tenon Made with Router

Blind Mortise and Haunched Tenon

Stile

Rail

Frame-and-Panel Haunched Tenon

Blind Mortise and Barefaced Tenon

Stile

Rail

Frame-and-Panel Stub Tenon

Blind Mortise-and-Tenon Joints

Illus. 9-3. Blind mortises are used when you want to hide the joint.

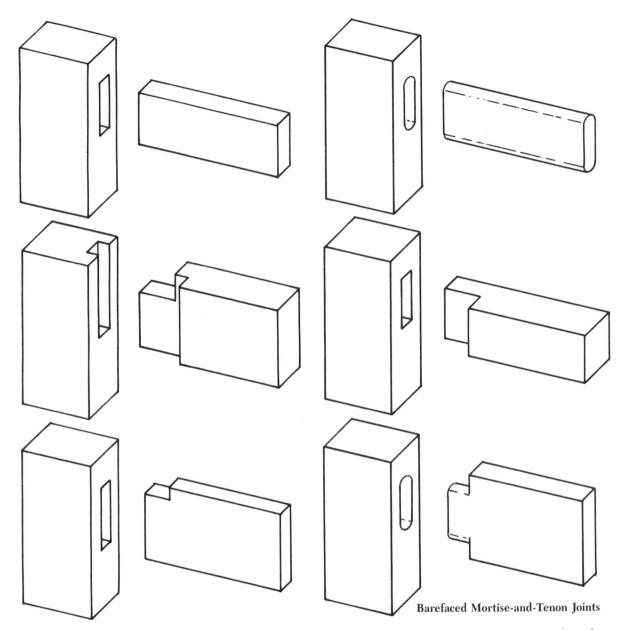

Barefaced Mortise-and-Tenon Joints

Illus. 9-4. Barefaced tenons are used when the tenon board is thinner than the mortise board. When the tenon board is thin, cutting a standard tenon would result in a tenon that is too thin to give the required strength. The barefaced tenon can be as thick as the tenon board, or you can cut a cheek on one side to bring the face of the tenon board flush with the face of the mortise board.

Making Mortise-and-Tenon Joints

Mortise-and-tenon joints can be made with hand or power tools. In this section, general directions are given for several ways of making mortise-and-tenon joints with power tools. On pages 98–101 are step-by-step directions for making mortise-and-tenon joints with hand tools.

Power-Tool Methods

Large shops use special machines to cut mortises, but for the small shop, the router is probably the best power tool to use. A plunge router and a shop-made jig make the job easy. Tenons can also be cut with a router that is used with a shop-made jig. (See Illus. 9-5.)

Illus. 9-5. The router can be used to make mortise-and-tenon joints. This joint was cut with a router. Note that the ends of the mortise are rounded. The tenon has been rounded with a file to match the mortise.

The tenons can be cut on the table saw. To do the job safely, use a tenoning jig. This is an accessory that fits into the mitre-gauge slot. It has clamps that will hold the work as the cuts are made. Open mortises can also be made with the table saw and a tenoning jig.

Mortising with a Router   A plunge router and the simple jig shown in Illus. 9-6 and 9-7 can be used to make mortises. To make the jig, start with a piece of ⅛-inch-thick hardboard that is about 6 inches wider than the diameter of the router base. The length of the hardboard should be equal to the diameter of the router base plus 6 inches plus the length of the mortise. Cut a strip of plywood or particleboard 3 inches wide and long enough to make four sides for the jig.

Attach the first side to the jig with glue and nails; then place the router on the jig and position the second side so that it just touches the router base. Slide the router to the other end of the jig and make sure that the side of the router is touching there. Mark the location and remove the router; then glue and nail the second side in place.

Cut a piece to fit between the two sides and attach it to the jig at one end; then place the router in the jig. Measure from the edge of the router base and mark the length of the mortise. Remove the router and attach the other end to the jig at that location.

Put the straight router bit being used to cut the mortise into the router. Place the jig on a piece of scrap and clamp it down. Position the router in the jig with the base butted against one end. Start the router and make a plunge cut through the hardboard. Cut across the jig until

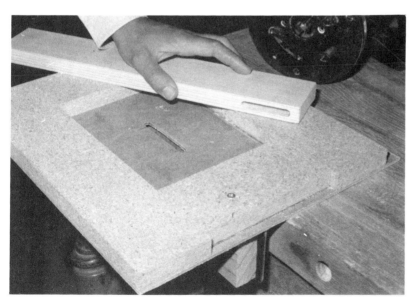

Illus. 9-6. This simple jig can be used to guide a router as you cut a mortise. It is designed to be used with a bench vise.

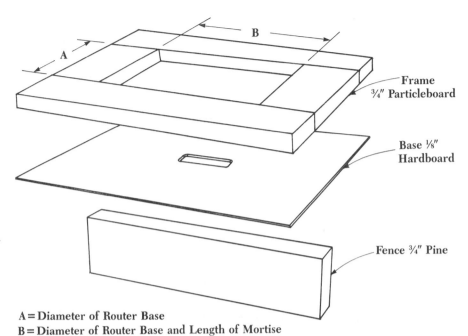

Illus. 9-7. An exploded view of the router mortising jig that shows its different parts. The size of the jig depends upon the size of your router and the size of mortise you will be making.

Frame
¾" Particleboard

Base ⅛"
Hardboard

Fence ¾" Pine

A = Diameter of Router Base
B = Diameter of Router Base and Length of Mortise

the router base hits the other end. You now have a cutout in the jig that is exactly the size of the mortise that this jig will make.

Now, attach a fence to the jig. Place the fence so that the mortise will be centered on the board. Attach it with screws driven down through the hardboard. Countersink the screw heads so that the router base won't get caught on them.

To cut the mortise, lay out the position of the mortise on the board. Set the plunge depth stop to the depth of the mortise plus ⅛ inch. Place the jig in a vise with the fence against the outside jaw of the vise. Place the board against the inside jaw and line up the layout marks on the board with the slot in the jig; then tighten the vise. (See Illus. 9-8.) You can make small adjustments to the position of the mortise by taping strips of paper or thin cardboard to the jig fence.

Place the router in the jig and start it. Lower the bit about ¼ inch into the board and cut across from one end of the jig to the other; then lower the bit ¼ inch more and make another pass. Repeat this procedure until you hit the depth stop. (See Illus. 9-9.)

Before removing the board from the vise, note that the mortise now has round ends. At this point, you can leave the ends round and round the tenon to match, or you can square up the ends with a chisel.

Illus. 9-8. Clamp the jig and the board to be mortised in the vise. Line up the layout marks on the board with the hole in the jig base. If the board isn't centered, you can make small adjustments by taping paper or cardboard shims to the jig fence.

Tenons with a Router The router can be used to cut a tenon in a single step. The same straight bit that was used to cut the mortise is used to make the tenon. To cut tenons with a router, you will need to make a jig similar to the one used to cut mortises. (See Illus. 9-10 and 9-11.) It will only cut one size of tenon, but since it is easy to make, you can make several different sizes. Making the jig is very similar to the process described for making the mortise jig.

Begin with a piece of ⅛-inch-thick hardboard. The width of the hardboard should be equal to the diameter of the router base plus the thickness of the tenon plus the diameter of the router bit

Illus. 9-9. To use the jig, place a plunge-cut router in the opening on top of the jig. The router base rubs against both sides of the jig, so it will make a straight cut. Start with the router at one end of the jig, lower the bit into the wood about ¼ inch, and then pull the router across to the other end of the jig. Lower the bit some more and make additional passes until the mortise is at the required depth.

Illus. 9-10. This jig will allow you to make tenons with the router. It is similar to the one used to make mortises. You can make a matched set of these jigs to cut mating mortises and tenons.

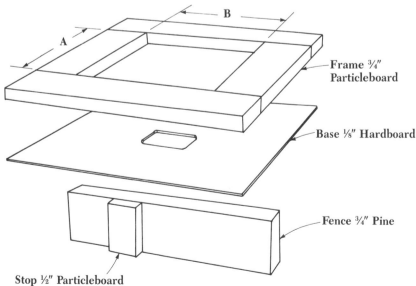

Frame ¾″ Particleboard

Base ⅛″ Hardboard

Fence ¾″ Pine

Stop ½″ Particleboard

A = Diameter of Router Base and Tenon Thickness and Diameter of Bit
B = Diameter of Router Base and Width of Tenon and Diameter of Bit

Illus. 9-11. This exploded view of the router tenoning jig shows how the jig is constructed. The size of the jig depends on the router and the size of the tenon. The main difference between this jig and the mortising jig, besides the dimensions, is the addition of a stop to the fence. The stop positions the tenon board and keeps it vertical.

plus 6 inches. The length of the hardboard is equal to the width of the tenon plus the diameter of the router base plus the diameter of the router bit plus 6 inches. You also need to cut a 3-inch-wide strip of particleboard to make the four side guides. (See Illus. 9-11.)

Attach the first side to the jig with glue and nails. Then place the router base on the jig with one side of the base touching the side of the jig. Make a mark on the hardboard at the opposite edge of the router base.

Next, measure the thickness of the tenon and the diameter of the router bit. Add these two measurements and make another mark on the hardboard base that is that much farther from the edge. This is the location of the other side guide. Attach the other side guide to the base, making sure that it is parallel with the first one.

Next, cut a piece to fit between the two sides, and attach it at one end. To find the location of the other end, add the diameter of the router base, the width of the tenon, and the diameter of the router bit, and measure that distance from the opposite end. Attach the end with glue and nails.

Now, clamp the jig to a piece of waste, and place the router on it. Start the router and make a plunge cut through the jig base. Cut around the jig with the router base always in contact with the side guides of the jig. You now have a hole in the jig that can be used to help position the board. This hole will be larger than the tenon, but you can use it to center the work. After cutting a test tenon, make marks on the jig to indicate exactly where to place the board.

Now, attach the fence. Position it so that the board to be tenoned will be centered in the hole in the base. Add a stop to the fence that will position the board so that the tenon width will be centered in the hole. The stop should be made of material that is thinner than the board, so it won't interfere with clamping.

To use the jig, place it in a vise with the fence against the outside jaw. (See Illus. 9-12.) Put a scrap board next to the inside jaw of the vise to keep the router bit from hitting the vise jaw. Place the board to be tenoned in the vise and

align it against the fence and stop. The end should be flush with the bottom of the jig base. To make this alignment easier, cut a small piece of ⅛-inch-thick hardboard that will fit inside the hole in the jig. Place it on top of the tenon board and move the board up and down until the hardboard insert is flush with the top of the jig base.

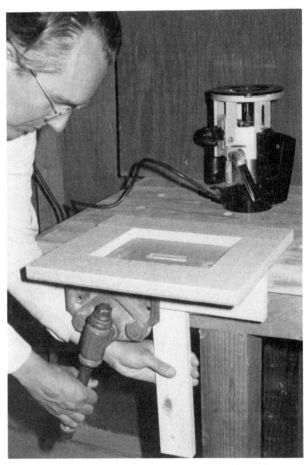

Illus. 9-12. Clamp the jig and the tenon board in the vise. A piece of scrap must be placed next to the inside jaw of the vise to prevent the router bit from hitting the vise jaw.

Set the plunge depth stop to the length of the tenon plus ⅛ inch. This is the same setting used to cut the mortise with the jig described earlier, so if you are using both jigs, you only need to set up the router once.

Place the router in the jig and press the sides of the router base tight into a corner of the jig.

Start the router and lower the bit into the wood. (See Illus. 9-13.) Short tenons can be cut in a single pass. Cut longer ones partway down in one pass, and then lower the bit to the stop to complete the tenon in another pass.

Illus. 9-13. Start the cut with the router in one corner of the jig. Lower the bit into the wood and cut around the tenon. Be sure to keep the router base against the jig guides at all times. Both side guides of the mortising jig should be in contact with the router base during the cut, so the router can't wander. The tenoning jig shown here, however, only has one side guide in contact with the router base at a time, so the router can wander away from the guide if the operator is not careful.

It is very important that the router base always touches the side guides of the jig as you make the cut. If the router strays away from the guide, the tenon will be nicked.

The tenon will have square corners when cut with this setup. If you want round corners to match a round-ended mortise, use a file to round the corners after you have cut the tenon.

Tenons with a Table Saw Tenons can also be cut on the table saw. You can make the tenon to fit any mortise, whether you make the mortise by hand, with a router, or make an open mortise with the table saw as described later.

To make a tenon safely on a table saw, it is best to have a tenon jig. This jig fits into the mitre-gauge slot of the table saw. The board being cut is clamped in place during the cutting.

Set up the jig according to the manufacturer's directions. Set the guides for the size board you are using, and then clamp the first board in place with its front face against the jig. (See Illus. 9-14.) Raise the blade until it touches the shoulder mark on the tenon. Adjust the tenon jig to cut the first cheek, and then make the cheek cut on all of the boards. Make sure that you always place each board in the jig with the board's front face against the jig.

Illus. 9-14. A tenoning jig fits into the mitre-gauge slot on a table saw. It has clamps and guides to hold the board in position safely as you cut tenons on the table saw. Adjust the jig to make the first side cheek cut, as shown here, and then cut the side cheeks on all of the tenons in the project.

Now, readjust the jig to make the second cheek cut. This cut is also made with the front face of the board against the jig. Using this procedure is more accurate than simply turning the board around in the jig. (See Illus. 9-15.)

If you need to make top or bottom cheek cuts, reposition the tenoning jig and make those cuts next. (See Illus. 9-16.)

After all of the cheek cuts are made, make the shoulder cuts using the mitre gauge. Clamp a stop block to the front part of the fence and adjust the fence position so that the board is correctly positioned to make the shoulder cut when its end is touching the stop block. The stop block

Illus. 9-15. You could use the same setup to cut the second side cheek by turning the board around, but the joint will be more accurate if you reset the tenoning jig and make the second cheek cut with the same face of the board against the jig. This will keep the front faces flush with the mortise board, and result in tenons that are all the same size, even if there is a slight variation in the thickness of the boards.

Illus. 9-16. The tenoning jig can be rotated to make the cuts for the top and bottom cheeks.

should be short enough so that the end of the board will be clear of the block before the cut begins.

Place the board on the table against the mitre gauge, and butt the board's end against the stop block. Hold the board firmly in position against the mitre gauge and advance the board into the saw. (See Illus. 9-17.) Repeat the procedure for all of the shoulder cuts.

Illus. 9-17. To make the shoulder cuts, use the mitre gauge as a guide. Place a stop block on the saw fence to help you position the board on the mitre gauge. Don't butt the end of the board against the fence without a stop block. If you make the cut with the end of the board in contact with the fence, the board may kick back.

You can also make tenons on the table saw using the dado blade. This method is not as accurate as that used with the tenoning jig, and the cheeks are rougher, but the results are acceptable for many applications. To set up the saw for this method, set the dado blade to the widest cut. Raise the blade to one-third the thickness of the board. Place a stop on the fence and adjust the fence position to make the shoulder.

Cut the top and bottom cheeks first. Place the board on the table saw with the board's face against the mitre gauge and its end against the stop. Advance the board into the blade. Hold the board firmly in position against the mitre gauge as you clear the stop. (See Illus. 9-18.)

After making the shoulder cut, reposition the board so that the next cut will slightly overlap the first. Make another pass over the blade to remove more of the waste. Keep repositioning the board and making passes across the blade until all of the waste is removed. Turn the board over and repeat the procedure to cut the cheek on the other side of the tenon.

The procedure for the side cheeks is similar. Place the board face down on the table saw with

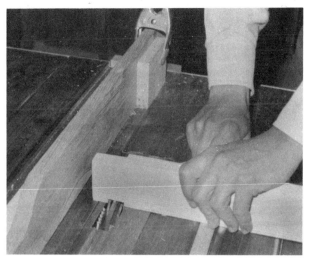

Illus. 9-18. The dado blade can also be used to cut tenons. Make the cuts for the top and bottom cheeks first, as shown here.

its edge against the mitre gauge, and butt the end of the board against the stop. Hold the board in position on the mitre gauge and advance it into the blade. (See Illus. 9-19.) After making the shoulder cut, reposition the board and make another pass to remove some of the waste. Make additional passes over the blade as necessary to remove all of the waste.

Illus. 9-19. To cut the side cheeks of a tenon with the dado blade, use the mitre gauge as a guide. Place a stop block on the fence to position the board for the shoulder cut. Make multiple passes to remove all of the waste.

Open Mortise with a Table Saw   An open mortise joint is easy to make on the table saw with a tenoning jig. The tenon is visible on the end and the edge of the mortise board when the joint is assembled. You can incorporate this type of joint into the design of the project and use it for decorative effect.

The open mortise is not quite as strong as other types of mortise-and-tenon joints, because the tenon can slip out of the joint in two directions. However, modern glues make the joint very strong, and it can be used in most applications.

To cut the mortise, set up the tenoning jig to hold the mortise board. Raise the blade to the width of the tenon board. In most cases, you will have to use a standard blade, because most dado blades won't be large enough to reach the required height. However, if the tenon board is not too wide, you may be able to make the mortise in a single pass using the dado blade.

To make the cut with a standard blade, set the tenoning jig to cut the first side of the mortise. Make the cut on all of the mortises in the project, and then change the jig setting to make the second side cut. After making that cut, make additional passes if necessary to remove the waste between the two cuts. (See Illus. 9-20.)

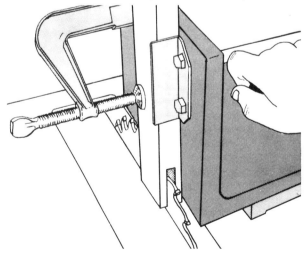

Illus. 9-20. The tenoning jig can be used to make an open mortise. The procedure is similar to making the cheek cuts on the tenon, but you make multiple cuts to remove the wood from the center of the board.

When assembling this joint, be sure to cover the joint completely with glue. This joint relies on a good glue bond for its strength. Assemble the joint, and then clamp across the joint to press the sides of the mortise against the cheeks of the tenon. (See Illus. 9-21.)

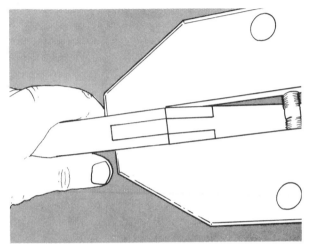

Illus. 9-21. When assembling an open mortise joint, clamp across the joint to make sure that the sides of the mortise are pressed firmly against the cheeks of the tenon. This joint relies on a good glue bond for its strength, so clamping is essential.

Mortise-and-Tenon Joint with Hand Tools

The traditional way to make mortise-and-tenon joints is to chop the mortise with a mortising chisel and cut the tenon with a standard back-saw. If you enjoy working with hand tools, making your joints by hand can be a rewarding experience.

Chopping the mortise with a chisel is an efficient way to make a mortise. Once you develop experience with this method, you can make mortises about as quickly as you can with power equipment. Cutting the tenon is a little more difficult and time-consuming, but it can be mastered by most beginners with a little practice.

Layout The first step in making a mortise-and-tenon joint is the layout. To lay out the joint for hand tools, you will need a sharp knife, a marking gauge, and a square. (See Illus. 9-22.)

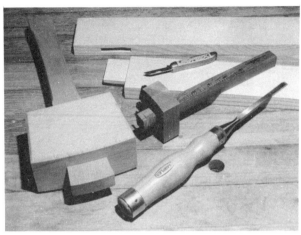

Illus. 9-22. To lay out the joint for hand tools you will need a sharp knife, a marking gauge, and a square.

Lay out the mortise and tenon at the same time. Always make them as a matched set. Number the joints so that you are aware where they belong while you are working. Place the parts together in the position they will be when assembled. Mark the front face on each board and make all gauged lines from the front face. Set the marking gauge to one-third the thickness of the mortised board. Gauge a line for the side of the mortise. The fence of the marking gauge should be against the front face.

With the same setting, gauge lines on the two edges and the end of the tenon board. (See Illus. 9-23.) Now, reset the marking gauge to two-thirds the thickness of the mortised board, and then mark the other side of the mortise with the gauge fence against the front face. Also mark the second set of lines on the tenon boards using this setting.

Measure the location of the mortise; leave about one inch of extra wood between the end of the board and the mortise location. This is called a horn. It helps to keep the board from splitting as you chop the mortise. The horn is trimmed flush with the tenon board after assembly.

Place a square against the board and use a sharp knife to mark the ends of the mortise. Measure the location of the shoulder cut on the tenon. Use a square to guide the knife as you mark the shoulder. Make two passes over the shoulder marks to make a deep cut. The knife cut will sever the wood fibres and make the shoulder cut clean and free of splinters. (See Illus. 9-24.)

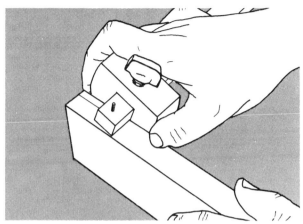

Illus. 9-23. Use a marking gauge to lay out the joint. Mark the front face on each board, and make all gauged lines from the front face. Set the marking gauge to one-third the thickness of the mortised board. Gauge a line for the side of the mortise. The fence of the marking gauge should be against the front face. With the same setting, gauge lines on the two edges and the end of the tenon board. Then re-set the marking gauge to two-thirds of the thickness of the mortised board, and mark the other side of the mortise with the gauge fence against the front face. Also mark the second set of lines on the tenon boards using this setting.

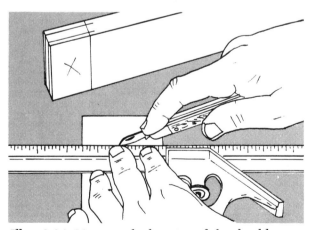

Illus. 9-24. Measure the location of the shoulder cut on the tenon. Use a square to guide the knife as you mark the shoulder. Make two passes over the shoulder marks to make a deep cut. The knife cut will sever the wood fibres and make the shoulder cut clean and free of splinters.

Chopping a Mortise   Place the board on a solid work surface. The area directly over a leg on the workbench is the sturdiest part of the bench. Clamp the work to the bench top. Don't put the board in a vise; the repeated blows with the mallet will loosen the vise.

Wrap a piece of masking tape around the chisel to indicate the depth of the mortise. Start the cut with the chisel about ⅛ inch in from the end of the mortise layout lines. The bevel on the chisel should face the opposite end of the mortise. Hold the chisel away from your body so that you can sight along it. The chisel has to be straight up and down in both directions.

Hit the handle of the chisel with a mallet. You should be able to drive the chisel about ½ inch into the wood with one blow. (See Illus. 9-25.) Reposition the chisel about ⅜ inch past the first location and hit it again. (See Illus. 9-26.) Keep repositioning the chisel and driving it in about ½ inch deep until you get close to the other end. Place the chisel bevel down into the mortise and

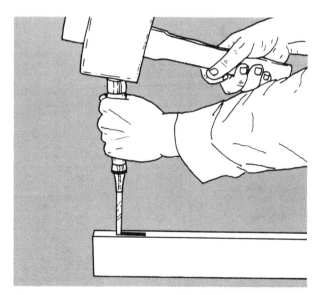

Illus. 9-25. Place the board on a solid work surface. Start the cut with the chisel about ⅛ inch in from the end of the mortise layout lines. The bevel on the chisel should face the opposite end of the mortise. Hold the chisel away from your body so that you can sight along it. The chisel should be straight up and down in both directions. Hit the handle of the chisel with a mallet. You should be able to drive the chisel about ½ inch into the wood with one blow.

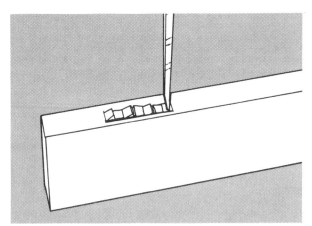

Illus. 9-26. Reposition the chisel about ⅜ inch past the first location and hit it again. Keep repositioning the chisel and driving it in about ½ inch deep until you get close to the other end.

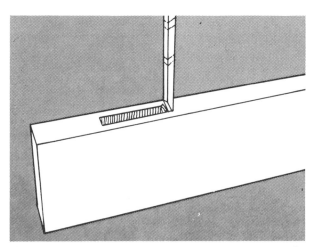

Illus. 9-28. After you have chopped to the required depth, place the chisel on the layout line for one end and drive it all the way to the bottom of the mortise. Turn the chisel around and repeat this procedure for the other end.

lever out the waste chips. (See Illus. 9-27.) Repeat the procedure, driving ½ inch deeper each time, until you reach the correct depth.

After you have chopped to the required depth, place the chisel on the layout line for one end and drive it all the way to the bottom of the mortise. Turn the chisel around and repeat this procedure for the other end. (See Illus. 9-28.)

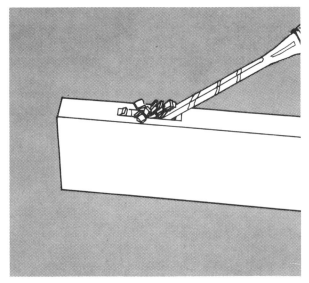

Illus. 9-27. Place the chisel bevel down into the mortise and lever out the waste chips. Repeat this procedure, driving ½ inch deeper each time until you reach the correct depth.

Cutting Tenons with a Backsaw Place the board in a vise end up and at approximately a 45-degree angle. Put the saw on the end of the board and line it up with the layout line; keep all of the saw kerf on the waste side of the line. Use your thumb against the saw blade to steady the saw.

Start the cut flat across the end. Once you have cut down about ⅛ inch, reposition the saw so that it is parallel to the bench top. Saw straight down, following the layout line, until you reach the shoulder mark. (See Illus. 9-29.) Before you reposition the board, repeat the same procedure for the other cheek.

Next, turn the board around and place the saw in the kerf on the end of the board. Start sawing; follow the visible layout line. Cut straight down until you reach the shoulder mark. Repeat the same procedure for the other cheek.

Now, place the board in the vise straight up. Put the saw in one of the kerfs. Saw down until you reach the shoulder mark. (See Illus. 9-30.) Do the same with the other kerf. If you are making a tenon with top and bottom cheeks, cut them now. Cut straight down the layout line.

Cut the shoulders in a mitre box. Place the saw so that the teeth just barely touch the line made with the knife, and then saw down to the cheek. (See Illus. 9-31.)

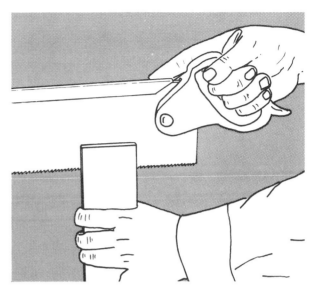

Illus. 9-29. *Place the board in a vise end up and at approximately a 45-degree angle. Put the saw on the end of the board and line it up with the layout line; keep all of the saw kerf on the waste side of the line. Use your thumb against the saw blade to steady the saw. Start the cut flat across the end. Once you have cut down about ⅛ inch, reposition the saw so that it is parallel to the bench top. Saw straight down, following the layout line until you reach the shoulder mark. Before repositioning the board, repeat the same procedure for the other cheek. Turn the board around and repeat this procedure following the other layout line.*

Illus. 9-30. *Place the board straight up in the vise and put the saw in one of the kerfs. Saw down until you reach the shoulder mark. Do the same with the other kerf.*

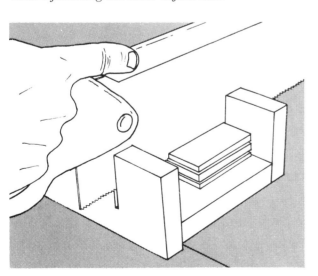

Illus. 9-31 *(left). Cut the shoulders in a mitre box. Place the saw so that the teeth just barely touch the line made with the knife, and then saw down to the cheek.*

Chapter 10

BOX JOINTS

As the name implies, box joints are a case joint usually used to make boxes. (See Illus. 10-1.) Many commercial boxes made in the 1800s and early 1900s had box joints. The box joint was developed as an alternative to the dovetail joint that could be cut easily by mass-production machinery.

The box joint is also called a finger joint because of the multiple fingers called pins that fit into notches called sockets. (See Illus. 10-2.) The strength of this joint comes from the large glue-surface area.

When to Use Box Joints

Box joints are usually used when you want to reproduce an antique. They were commonly used to make the cases for sewing machines, telephones, scientific instruments, coffee grinders, and butter moulds, and to make packing crates. Box joints can be used in other case-joint applications, usually for decorative effect.

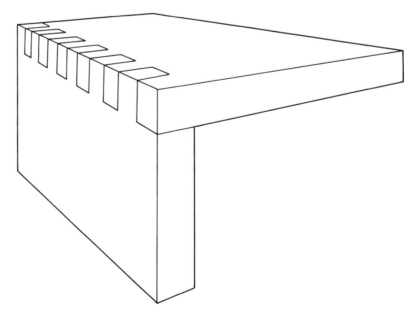

Illus. 10-1. Box joint.

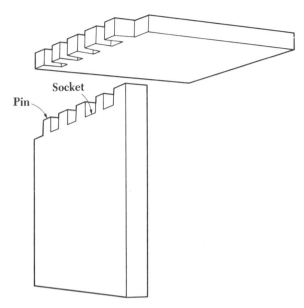

Illus. 10-2. The box joint is also called a finger joint because of the multiple fingers called pins that fit into notches called sockets.

Making Box Joints

Box joints were developed as a machine joint, so they are not usually made by hand. Mass-production equipment can make the joint in a single pass, but in small shops the joint is usually made with multiple passes on a table saw. Commercially available jigs can be used to position the cuts, but a simple shop-made jig is used by most woodworkers. (See Illus. 10-3.) The size of the pins can be varied, but three proportions of pins are often used: pins one-half the thickness of the board, one-fourth the thickness of the board, or equal to the thickness of the board. (See Illus. 10-4.) The pins are usually made a little longer than necessary, so that you can trim them flush after assembly. A few passes with a belt sander will trim the pins flush and create a nice-looking joint.

A strong glue bond is important to a strong joint. Drip a little glue into each socket and spread it inside the socket with a small stiff brush.

The order in which you cut the joints is not important, if you don't mind that the sockets and pins on one end of the board may not line up with the ones on the other end. If you do want the joints that are opposite each other to line up, then you need to follow a specific order as you cut the joints. For the purpose of describing the procedure, the parts of a box and each corner joint in Illus. 10-5 have been labelled. These letters and numbers will be referred to in the following directions.

Begin by making the jig. Cut a piece of wood and attach it to the mitre gauge with clamps. The size of the mitre-gauge extension depends upon the size of the parts you will be making. Make the extension large enough to provide adequate support to the parts as you cut the joints. The

Illus. 10-3. This simple shop-made jig can be used to make box joints on the table saw.

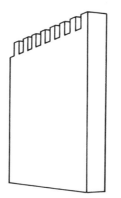 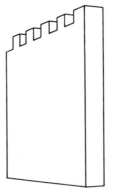 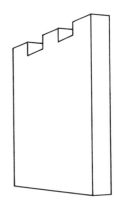

Illus. 10-4. *The three standard proportions for the pins are: one-fourth the thickness of the board, one-half the thickness of the board, or equal to the thickness of the board.*

One-Fourth-Thickness Pins   **One-Half-Thickness Pins**   **Equal Pins**

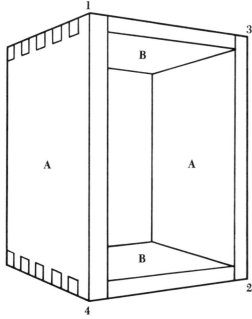

Illus. 10-5. *For the purpose of describing the procedure, the parts of a box and each corner joint are labelled here. These letters and numbers will be referred to in the directions in the text.*

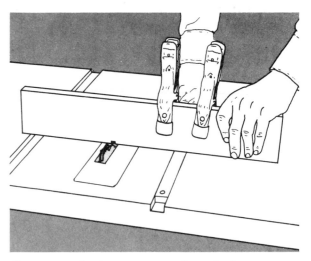

Illus. 10-6. *The first step in making the box joint jig is to use the dado blade to cut a notch in a wood extension clamped to the mitre gauge.*

directions given here are for ¼-inch-wide pins cut on a ¼-inch-thick board. You must remove the blade guard on the table saw to use this jig, so be careful when using the saw and keep your fingers well away from the blade.

Install the dado blade on the table saw, and set it to make a ¼-inch-wide cut. Raise the blade to ³⁄₁₆ inch to make the jig; later, when you cut the joint, the blade will be raised more. Turn on the saw and cut a notch in the wood mitre-gauge extension. (See Illus. 10-6.)

Remove the wood extension from the mitre gauge and cut a hardwood key to fit in the notch. In this example, the size of the key is ¼ × ³⁄₁₆ × 1 inch. Glue the key into the notch with the key projecting from the front of the jig. (See Illus. 10-7.) After the glue is dry, round the top of the key with sandpaper. This will make it easier to slip the sockets over the key as you cut the joint. You now have a completed box-joint jig.

Now, place the jig against the mitre gauge and position it so that the key is exactly ¼ inch away from the blade. Clamp the jig to the mitre gauge and make a test cut. If the position is correct, attach the jig to the fence with screws.

The jig is now ready to be used. Raise the dado blade to ⁹⁄₃₂ inch. This will make pins that are ¹⁄₃₂

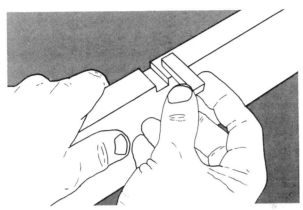

Illus. 10-7. Cut a hardwood key to fit in the notch. In this example, the size of the key is ¼ × ³⁄₁₆ × 1 inch. Glue the key into the notch with the key projecting from the front of the jig.

inch longer than necessary, to allow you to sand them flush after assembly. The sides and joints are referred to according to the letters and numbers shown in Illus. 10-5. Begin with side A. Place it on the saw with its outside face against the jig and the end marked 1 against the saw table. Butt the edge against the key. Hold the board firmly in place. Spring clamps can be used to hold the board in position as you make the cut. Turn on the saw and make the first cut. (See Illus. 10-8.)

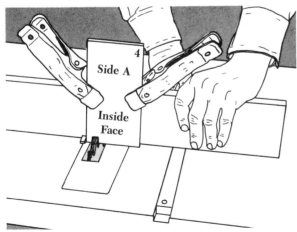

Illus. 10-8. Begin cutting the joint on side A. (Refer to Illus. 10-5.) Place it on the saw with its outside face against the jig and the end marked 1 against the saw table. Butt its edge against the key. Hold the board firmly in place. Spring clamps can be used to hold the board in position as you make the cut.

To make the next socket, place the first socket over the key and clamp the board in place. Cut the next socket. (See Illus. 10-9.) Now, reposition the board, again placing the socket you just cut over the key. Continue in this manner until you reach the end of the joint.

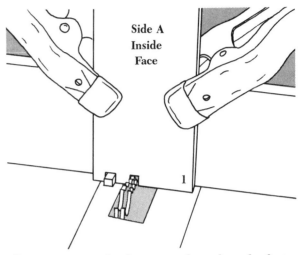

Illus. 10-9. To make the next socket, place the first socket over the key and clamp the board in place. To cut the remainder of the sockets, reposition the board, placing the socket you just cut over the key.

Next, cut the sockets in side B. Use side A to position side B for the first cut. Place side A on the jig with its inside face against the jig; this is the reverse of the position side A was in when it was being cut. Place the first socket on side A over the key. Place side B with its inside face against the jig, the end marked 1 against the saw table, and the edge butted against the edge of side A. Now, cut the first socket in side B. (See Illus. 10-10.)

After you have cut the first socket, remove side A from the jig. Place the first notch in side B over the key in the jig and cut the second socket. (See Illus. 10-11.) Reposition the board, as you did previously, to cut the rest of the sockets.

Repeat the above directions for joint number 2. This is the joint diagonally opposite joint number one. To cut joint numbers 3 and 4, do the following: Place side A with its inside face against the jig. Butt the edge of side A against the key and make the first socket cut.

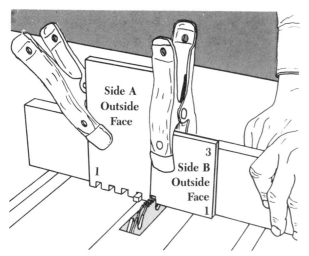

Illus. 10-10. Use side A to position side B for the first cut. Place side A on the jig with its inside face against the jig. Place the first socket on side A over the key. Place side B with its inside face against the jig, the end marked 1 against the saw table, and its edge butted against the edge of side A.

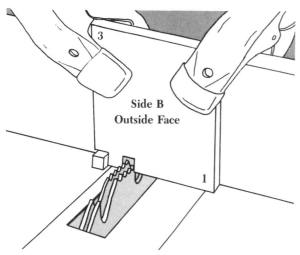

Illus. 10-11. After you have cut the first socket, remove side A from the jig. Place the first notch in side B over the key in the jig and cut the second socket. Reposition the board to cut the rest of the sockets.

Reposition the board to make the remainder of the sockets as described earlier, and then place side B on the jig. Use part A to position the first socket in side B as you did before, but this time place side A with its outside face against the jig. After cutting the first socket, remove side A and cut the rest of the sockets in side B as described above. (See Illus. 10-12.)

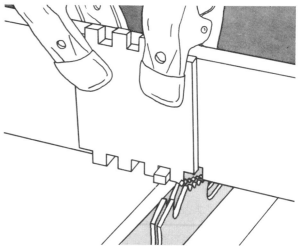

Illus. 10-12. The rest of the joints are cut in the same way, but refer to the directions to determine which face of the board should be placed against the fence.

Use sandpaper to smooth any splintering or rough areas on the joints. Make a test assembly before you apply glue to the joint. (See Illus. 10-13.) If necessary, make small adjustments with a file. Apply glue to the joint, and assemble it.

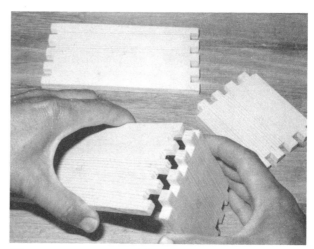

Illus. 10-13. Test-assemble the joint. You can make small adjustments with a file.

Chapter 11

DOVETAIL JOINTS

Dovetails are a case joint. Tapered pins fit into sockets between flared tails. (See Illus. 11-1.) The dovetail joint is one of the strongest of the case joints. Because the parts interlock, the joint provides mechanical strength besides the strength of the large glue-surface area. A well-made dovetail can be decorative as well as functional.

There are a variety of types of dovetails. In this chapter the two most basic types are covered: the through dovetail and the half-blind dovetail. If you are interested in other types, consult the *Wood Joiner's Handbook*.

both boards. When you want the joint to be visible as part of the design of the project, use a through dovetail. Through dovetails are often used to make boxes and chests.

The tail sockets of a *half-blind dovetail* are only cut part of the way through the pin board; this conceals the joint on one face, but the joint is still visible on the face of the other board. Use the half-blind joint when strength is the main consideration, but you don't want the joint to show as part of the design of the project. The half-blind dovetail is most often used in drawer construction.

When to Use Dovetails

Consider using dovetail joints when you are making a high-quality project that demands a lot of time and craftsmanship. Dovetails are usually used to make things such as boxes, drawers, cabinet carcasses, and chests.

The *through dovetail* is visible on the face of

Making Dovetails

Dovetail joints can be made with a handsaw and a chisel or with a router and a special jig. There are also ways to make dovetails with other types of power equipment and jigs. If you are interested in these methods, refer to the *Wood Joiner's Handbook*. Explored in this chapter are the basic ways to make through dovetails by hand and half-blind dovetails with a router jig.

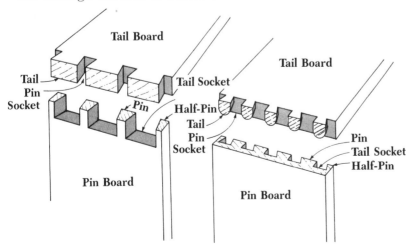

Tail Board

Tail Pin Socket

Tail Socket

Pin

Half-Pin

Tail Pin Socket

Pin Board

Tail Board

Pin

Tail Socket

Half-Pin

Pin Board

Illus. 11-1. Dovetails are a case joint used to join the end of one board to the face of another at a corner. Shown here are a through dovetail and a half-blind dovetail.

Hand-Cut Through Dovetails

Hand-cut through dovetails can be made in any size or spacing desired. In this example, let's assume that ¾-inch-thick lumber is being used, and that the pins being made will be ¾ inch wide at their widest point.

Making through dovetails by hand requires careful layout. You will need a marking gauge, a sliding T bevel, a square, and a knife. (See Illus. 11-2.)

Illus. 11-2. You will need these tools to lay out a through dovetail joint: a marking gauge, a sliding T bevel, a square, and a sharp knife.

Begin the layout with the marking gauge. Set the gauge to ⅟₃₂ inch more than the thickness of the wood. In this case the gauge setting is ²⁵⁄₃₂ inch. Gauge a line on both faces of the pin board and both faces and both edges of the tail board. (See Illus. 11-3.)

Next, lay out the position of the pins. The pins at the edges of the board are called half-pins because they are angled on only one side. The actual size of the half-pin is about the same as the rest of the pins.

The size and spacing of the pins is largely a matter of personal taste. Very small pins are nice-looking, but hard to make. Beginners are advised to make the widest part of the pin equal to the thickness of the board. The tail socket between the pins should be equal to or larger than the pin. You can vary the spacing as needed to get an even spacing between the pins on the board.

Illus. 11-3. Begin the layout with the marking gauge. Set the gauge to ⅟₃₂ inch more than the thickness of the wood. In this case, the gauge setting is ²⁵⁄₃₂ inch. Gauge a line on both faces of the pin board and both faces and both edges of the tail board.

In this example, four full pins and two half pins are being used. Use a pencil to make a line ⅜ inch away from the edge of the board along both edges. This represents the centerline of a ¾-inch-wide half pin.

Use the angled rule method to evenly space the rest of the pins. To use this method, place the rule with the zero indicator aligned with one of the half-pin centerlines. Now, pick a number that is greater than the width of the board and easily divided by the number of full pins plus one. (You can remember this easily if you think that the two half pins count as one full pin for this calculation.)

In this example, the board is 8 inches wide and there are four full pins, so 10 will be the number used. Angle the rule until 10 lines up with the other half-pin centerline. Since 10 divided by 5 is 2, make a mark every two inches. (See Illus. 11-4.)

Next, transfer the marks to the end of the board. Place a square against the end of the board and line its blade up with the mark. Make a new mark at the end of the board. (See Illus. 11-5.) Each of these marks represents the centerline of the pin. Since these pins will be ¾ inch wide, measure out from the centerline ⅜ inch on both sides.

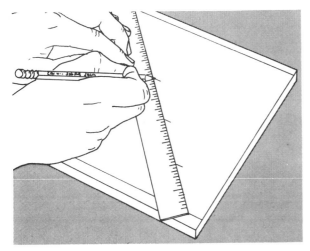

Illus. 11-4. *Next, lay out the position of the pins. Use a pencil to make a line ⅜ inch away from the edge of the board along both edges. This represents the centerline of a ¾-inch-wide half-pin. Use the angled rule method to get the rest of the pins evenly spaced. Place the rule with the zero indicator aligned with one of the half-pin centerlines. Now, pick a number that is greater than the width of the board and easily divided by the number of full pins plus one. Angle the rule until that number lines up with the other half-pin centerline. Now, mark the location of the pins.*

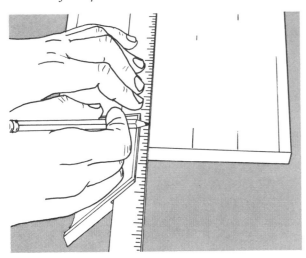

Illus. 11-5. *Transfer the marks to the end of the board. Place a square against the end of the board and line up its blade with the mark. Make a mark at the end of the board.*

Now, set the sliding T bevel. In this example, pine is being used, so use a slope of 1:6. If you were using a hardwood, you could use a 1:8 slope. On a piece of scrap, measure 1 inch from the corner along the end and 6 inches from the corner along the edge. Line up the blade of the bevel with these marks and tighten the wing nut. (See Illus. 11-6.)

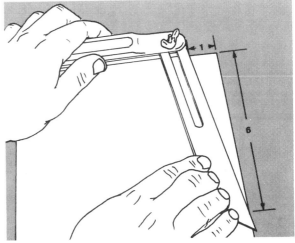

Illus. 11-6. *Now, set the sliding T bevel. In this illustration, a slope of 1:6 is being used. On a piece of scrap, measure 1 inch from the corner along the end and 6 inches from the corner along the edge. Line up the blade of the bevel with these marks and tighten the wing nut.*

Place the sliding T bevel on the end of the pin board and use a sharp knife to mark the sides of the pins. (See Illus. 11-7.) Use a square to con-

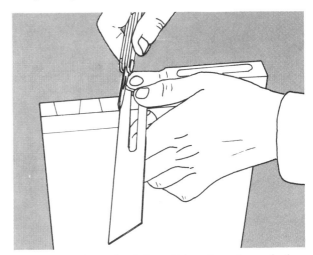

Illus. 11-7. *Place the sliding T bevel on the end of the pin board and use a sharp knife to mark the sides of the pins, as shown here. Then use a square to continue the lines down to the shoulder mark.*

tinue the lines down to the shoulder mark. Use a knife to make these marks. With a pencil, make an X in the waste area between the pins. This will help prevent confusion as you cut the joint.

Now, cut the pins. Place the board end up in a vise. Place the fine-toothed backsaw flat on the end of the board and line up its teeth with the layout line. The teeth should just barely touch the line, and all of the kerf should be in the waste area. Hold your thumb against the blade to steady it as you start the cut. Cut straight down to the shoulder line, and then stop and move to the next cut. (See Illus. 11-8.)

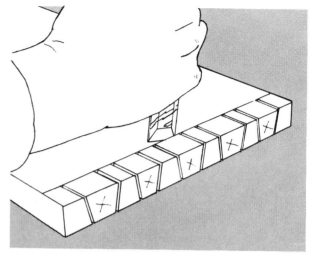

Illus. 11-9. Remove the board from the vise and lay it flat on the workbench. Then use the corner of a chisel to score along the shoulder line in the waste areas marked with an X, as shown here.

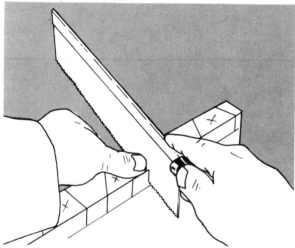

Illus. 11-8. To cut the pins, place the board end up in a vise. Place the saw flat on the end of the board and line up its teeth with the layout line. The teeth should just barely touch the line, and all of the kerf should be in the waste. Hold your thumb against the blade to steady it as you start the cut. Cut straight down to the shoulder line, and then stop and move to the next cut.

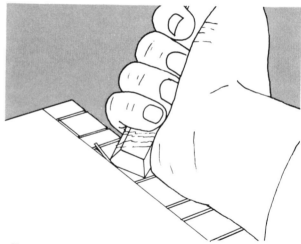

Illus. 11-10. Next, hold the chisel at an angle and make a shallow sloping cut into the shoulder. This will make the visible shoulder line sharp and splinter-free.

Now, lay the board flat on the workbench. Use the corner of a sharp chisel to score along the shoulder line in the waste areas marked with an X. (See Illus. 11-9.) Next, hold the chisel at an angle and make a shallow sloping cut into the shoulder. This will make the visible shoulder line sharp and splinter-free. (See Illus. 11-10.)

Now, clamp the board down and start to chop out the waste. Place the chisel blade on the shoulder line and drive it in about ⅛ inch. Do

this for all of the shoulder cuts on this face of the board. (See Illus. 11-11.)

Next, place the chisel on the end of the board and drive it in to split out the waste. When you have removed the first chip from each of the sockets, repeat the procedure, driving the chisel ⅛ inch deeper into the shoulder and then splitting out another chip. After cutting halfway through, turn the board over and repeat the process on the other face. (See Illus. 11-12.)

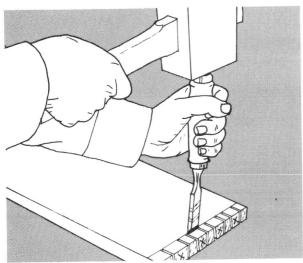

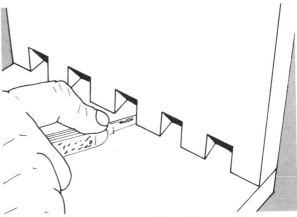

Illus. 11-11. Now, clamp the board to the bench and start to chop out the waste. Place the chisel blade on the shoulder line and drive it in about ⅛ inch. Do this for all of the shoulder cuts on this face of the board.

Illus. 11-13. Lay out the tail board using the pin board as a guide. Place the pin board on the inside face of the tail board and line it up with the shoulder line. Use a knife to trace around each pin. Use a square to transfer the marks to the end of the board.

board. Angle the saw to match the angle of the tail. Hold your thumb against the saw to steady it as you start the cut. Saw down along the line. Make sure that the kerf is entirely in the waste area. Stop the cut when you reach the shoulder line. Move the saw to the next location and repeat the procedure. (See Illus. 11-14.)

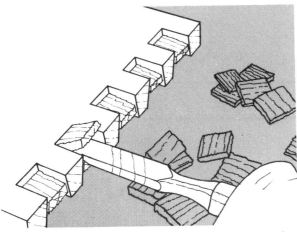

Illus. 11-12. To split out the waste, place the chisel on the end of the board and drive it in. After cutting halfway through, turn the board over and repeat the process on the other face.

Lay out the tail board using the pin board as a guide. Place the pin board on the inside face of the tail board and line it up with the gauge's shoulder line. Use a sharp knife to trace around each pin. (See Illus. 11-13.) Use a square to transfer the marks to the end of the board.

Now, saw out the tails. Mark an X in the waste. Place the tail board end up in a vise and place the saw with its teeth flat against the end of the

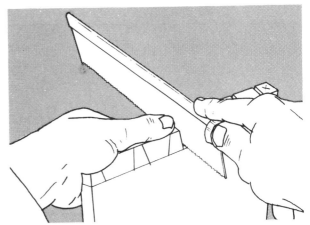

Illus. 11-14. To saw out the tails, place the tail board end up in a vise, and place the saw with its teeth flat against the end of the board. Angle the saw to match the angle of the tail. Hold your thumb against the saw to steady it as you start the cut. Saw down along the line. Make sure that the kerf is entirely in the waste area. Stop the cut when you reach the shoulder line. Move the saw to the next location and repeat the procedure.

Reposition the board in the vise and saw down the shoulder line to remove the waste from the half-pin sockets. (See Illus. 11-15.) Using the same procedure given for the pins, chop out the waste between the tails with a chisel. Chop down along the shoulder line first. (See Illus. 11-16.) Drive the chisel in from the end to split out a chip of wood in the pin socket. (See Illus. 11-17.)

Test-fit the joint. If it fits well, don't assemble

Illus. 11-17. Drive the chisel in from the end to split out a chip of waste.

it completely or you may damage it as you disassemble it; just assemble it far enough to determine that it will fit properly. (See Illus. 11-18.) If you need to, you can make adjustments with a chisel.

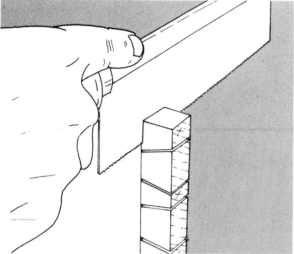

Illus. 11-15. Reposition the board in the vise and saw down the shoulder line to remove the waste from the half-pin sockets.

Illus. 11-18. Test-fit the joint. If it fits well, don't drive it all the way together or you may damage it as you disassemble it; just assemble it enough to determine that it will fit properly. If you need to, make adjustments with a chisel.

Now, cut the rest of the joints in the project. You don't need to lay out the rest of the joints with the bevel. Use the marking gauge to make the shoulder line; then place the previously cut pin board against the end of the next board and trace around the pins with a knife.

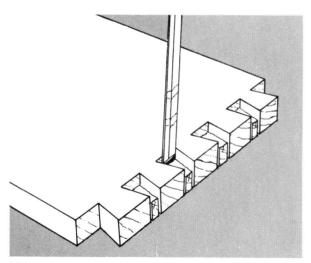

Illus. 11-16. Using the same procedure given for the pins, chop out the waste between the tails with a chisel. Begin by scoring the shoulder with the edge of the chisel. Then chop in 1/8 inch along the shoulder line.

When you have cut the new set of pins, use them to lay out the mating tail board. Always use the mating pin board to lay out the tail board so that you will compensate for any variations in the way you cut the pins.

When all of the joints are made, assemble the project. Apply glue to the inside of the sockets on both boards. Assemble the boards and clamp if necessary. Place blocks of wood that fit between the pins between the clamp jaws and the tail board.

If there are gaps in the joint, fill them by inserting a thin piece of wood. Split the piece from a scrap with a chisel. Place it in the gap while the glue is still wet. (See Illus. 11-19.) If the glue has dried before you notice the gap, use the dovetail saw to saw a kerf along the gap; then put some glue in the gap and insert the filler. A small piece of wood veneer can be used in this case.

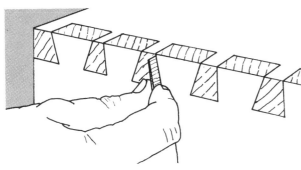

Illus. 11-19. If there are gaps in the joint, fill them with a small piece of wood split from a scrap with a chisel.

Half-Blind Dovetails with a Router

A router jig of the type shown in Illus. 11-20 is often used to make drawer joints. It is one of the least-expensive types, and will work with boards up to 8 inches wide. If you plan on making wider joints, there are larger jigs available. (See Illus. 11-21.) If you will be using the jig a lot, a heavy-duty jig may be necessary.

The exact setup for the jig varies from jig to jig. Consult the directions that come with the jig for exact instructions. The steps shown here are the general steps that most jigs require.

There are three types of drawer fronts that can be used with this least-expensive jig. (See Illus. 11-22.) The drawer front can be flush with the side or be set to make a small lip or a larger lip.

Begin by installing a template-following collar on the router and then inserting a dovetail bit in the chuck. (See Illus. 11-23.) Make a test joint on scrap to check the setup. Begin with the router bit ½ inch out from the base. Make the test cut and assemble the joint. If it is too loose, lower the bit about ¹⁄₃₂ inch; if it is too tight, raise the bit ¹⁄₃₂ inch.

Once you have a joint that fits well, save it for future setup. To adjust the depth of cut, place the sample joint in the jig. Put the router on the jig and adjust the depth of cut until the bottom of the bit lines up with the bottom of the cut in the sample joint.

When the jig is completely set up, cut the

Illus. 11-20. This is an inexpensive jig that is used to make half-blind dovetails. Jigs of this type are usually used for making drawers. The drawer front is placed under the template on the top of the jig, and the drawer side is clamped to the front of the jig. Pins and tails are cut in a single operation.

Illus. 11-21. This heavy-duty jig operates on the same principles as the inexpensive one, but you can use wider boards and the jig can withstand a lot of heavy use.

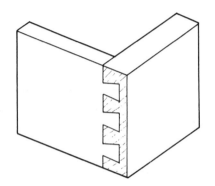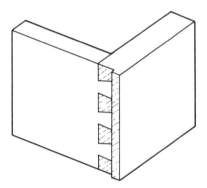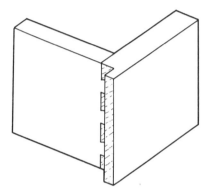

Illus. 11-22. The dovetail jig can be set to make these three types of drawer fronts. The flush joint at left is used when the drawer front is flush with the cabinet and no clearance is needed for drawer guides. The small lip shown in the middle is used when more side clearance is needed, but the drawer front will still be flush with the cabinet. When the drawer front lips over the front of the cabinet, the lipped joint shown on the right is used. This joint can also be used with a flush drawer front if you are using drawer guides that need ½-inch side clearance.

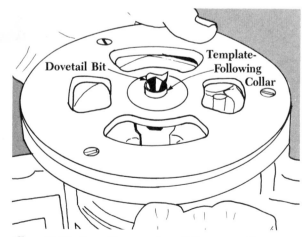

Illus. 11-23. Install a template-following collar on the router base before inserting the dovetail bit into the router. The collar will rub against the jig template and guide the cut.

parts to size. The size of the drawer front is not affected by the joint, but the sides are. Measure the tails on the test joint. Add this dimension to the length of the drawer sides. If you are also using a dovetail at the back of the drawer, add the necessary length for that joint also.

Now, place the parts in the jig. Place the drawer front on the top of the jig under the finger template. The finger template on the jig controls the joint layout. Align the end of the drawer front with the front of the jig and push its edge against the side guides. The inside face of the drawer front should be facing up.

Clamp the side to the front of the jig. The inside face of the side should be facing out. Butt the end of the drawer front against the bottom of the finger template and push its edge against the side guide. The jig guides are made to offset the side from the front the width of one pin. This makes it possible to cut the pins and tails in a single step. (See Illus. 11-24.)

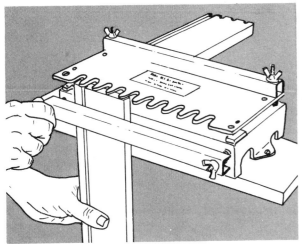

Illus. 11-24. Place the drawer front under the template on top of the jig. The inside of the drawer front should face up. Place the mating drawer side on the front of the jig under the clamping bar. The inside of the drawer side should face out. Note that the groove for the drawer bottom is visible from the front of the jig. This indicates that the parts are facing correctly.

Place the router base on top of the finger template. Always keep the router base flat against the template during the cut. Never lift the router from the base during the cut. If you do, you will damage the finger template.

Start the router and make a light cut across the board. This will help to minimize splintering. Now, start at the edge and cut the joint by following the finger template. The template-following collar will rub against the finger template and guide the cut. Keep the collar in contact with the template all during the cut. (See Illus. 11-25.)

After you have cut the joint, examine it before removing the parts from the jig. If wood chips build up in the template, they can prevent the collar from going all the way back. If it appears that some of the cuts are not as deep as others, clean the chips from the jig and make another pass with the router to make all of the sockets uniform.

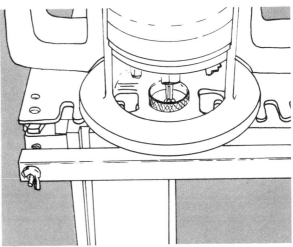

Illus. 11-25. Begin the cut by making a light pass across the front without following the template into the sockets. This will help prevent splintering as you make the next cut. Now, place the router so that the template-following collar is against the template, and cut into the sockets, as shown here. Keep the collar in constant contact with the template, and keep the router base flat against the top of the template.

Remove the boards from the jig and repeat the procedure for the next joint. Follow the instructions that come with the jig regarding the placement of the parts for joints on the opposite side of the drawer.

After all of the joints are cut, apply glue to the sockets and assemble the joint. (See Illus. 11-26.)

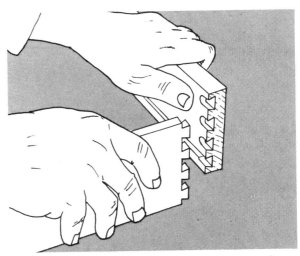

Illus. 11-26. When all of the joints are cut, apply glue to the sockets and assemble the joint.

Chapter 12

MAKING A JOINER'S BOX

The information provided in this chapter shows how to apply the joint-making techniques explored in prevous chapters to make a joiner's box. You don't need to build this project to benefit from this information, but building a joiner's box will provide you with an opportunity to make several important joints.

The design of this joiner's box is based on the boxes 19th-century woodworkers used to store their tools. (See Illus. 12-1.) The box described and shown in this chapter has been built with 1 × 12-inch pine. The dimensions used make it convenient to make, because you can use the full width of a 1 × 12 for the sides. The following joints are used to make the box: dovetails for the sides, mortise-and-tenon joints for the lid frame, a tongue-and-groove joint for the lid panel, blind dowels to join two boards to make the bottom, a barefaced tongue-and-groove joint to join the bottom to the sides, and a pegged joint to attach the handles.

Begin construction by cutting the sides (Part A) and the ends (Part B) to length. The length given for Part B in the Bill of Materials includes the length of the pins on Part B. Refer to Illus. 12-3 and 12-4 for the part labels used in these directions and shown in Illus. 12-2.

Next, cut the groove for the bottom. Set the dado blade on the table saw to make a ⅜-inch-wide × ⅜-inch-deep cut. Adjust the fence to place the cut ¾ inch from the edge of the board. Cut a groove on the inside face along the bottom edge of all four parts. (See Illus. 12-5.)

Now, lay out and cut the dovetails. (See Illus. 12-6.) Refer to the directions in Chapter 11. Part B is the pin board, and Part A the tail board. This way, the dovetail joint looks better from the front. Some of the original boxes of this type had the dovetails oriented the other way. You can make Part A the pin board, if you choose, without affecting any of the dimensions given in the plan.

The bottom (Part C) is wider than the width of a 1 × 12. Use a blind dowel joint to make up this

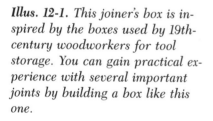

Illus. 12-1. This joiner's box is inspired by the boxes used by 19th-century woodworkers for tool storage. You can gain practical experience with several important joints by building a box like this one.

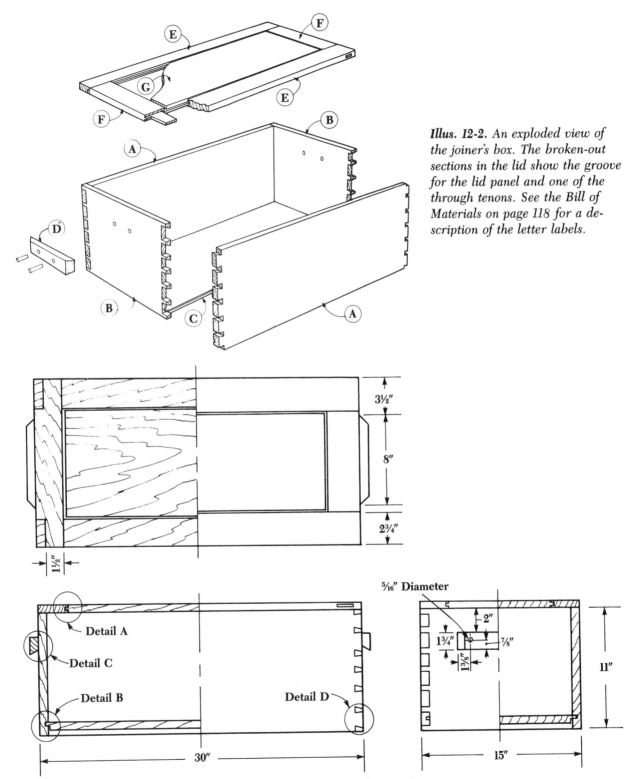

Illus. 12-2. An exploded view of the joiner's box. The broken-out sections in the lid show the groove for the lid panel and one of the through tenons. See the Bill of Materials on page 118 for a description of the letter labels.

Illus. 12-3. The top, front, and side views of the joiner's box. The wood-grain areas are shown in cross section. The top-view cross section shows the through tenons of the lid.

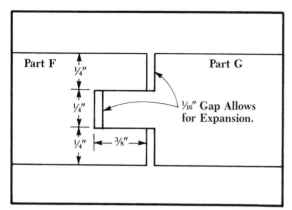

Detail A: Tongue on Panel "Floats" in Groove.
Do Not Glue.

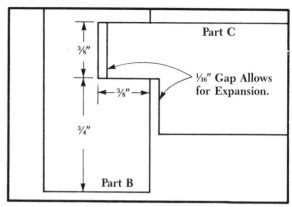

Detail B: Barefaced Tongue on Bottom "Floats" in
Groove in Side. Do Not Glue.

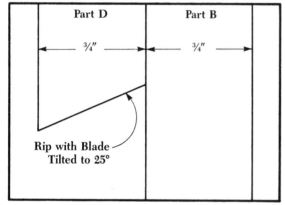

Detail C: Bottom of Handle is Cut at a 25° Angle
to Give a Better Grip.

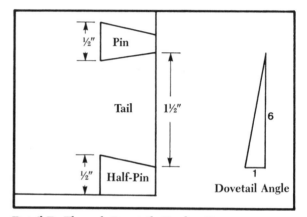

Detail D: Through Dovetails Used at Corners.
Five Full Pins and Two Half-Pins Used
in Example. You Can Vary Size and Spacing
if You Want.

Illus. 12-4. Details for the joiner's box.

JOINER'S BOX

BILL OF MATERIALS
(All material is 1″ pine, which is actually ¾″ thick.)

PART	DESCRIPTION	SIZE	NO. REQ'D
A	sides	11 × 30	2
B	ends	11 × 15	2
C	bottom	14⅛ × 29⅛	1
D	handles	1¾ × 8	2
E	lid stiles	2¾ × 30	2
F	lid rails	2¾ × 15	2
G	lid panel	10⅛ × 25⅛	1

Table 12-1.

panel. You can add a narrow strip to a full-width 1 × 12, as shown in Illus. 12-7, or make up the bottom from several narrow boards. Refer to Chapter 2 for dowel joint directions.

After you have glued up the bottom panel, cut a barefaced tongue on all four edges. Set the dado blade to make a cut wider than ⅜ inch. Attach an auxiliary wood fence to the saw fence. With the saw lowered below the table, adjust the fence so that ⅜ inch of the blade is exposed; then turn on the saw and raise the blade to ⅜ inch. The saw is now set up to cut the tongue. Place the bottom (Part C) with its outside face against the saw table. Cut a tongue on all four edges.

(See Illus. 12-8.) Refer to Chapter 6 for directions on making tongue-and-groove joints.

At this point, assemble the box. Apply glue to the first dovetail joint and put it together. (See Illus. 12-9.) Next, place the tongue of the bottom (Part C) in the grooves. Don't use any glue on

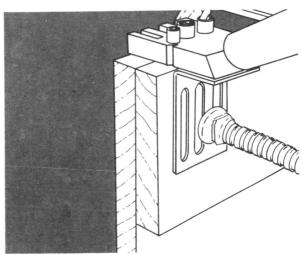

Illus. 12-7. The bottom (Part C) is 14⅛ inches wide. Use a blind dowel joint to add a 3⅛-inch-wide strip to a full width 1 × 12 to make the bottom. Refer to Chapter 2 for dowel joint directions.

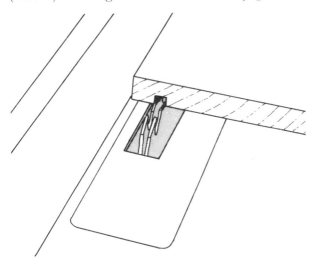

Illus. 12-5. Begin construction by cutting the sides (Part A) and the ends (Part B) to length. After the parts are cut to length, cut the groove for the bottom, as shown here. Set the dado blade to make a ⅜-inch-wide × ⅜-inch-deep cut. Adjust the fence to place the cut ¾ inch from the edge of the board. Cut a groove on the inside face along the bottom edge of all four parts.

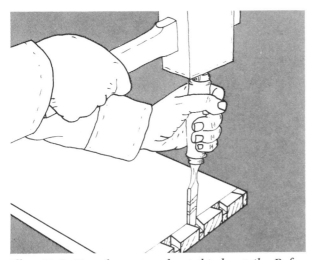

Illus. 12-6. Now, lay out and cut the dovetails. Refer to the directions in Chapter 11. Part B is the pin board, and Part A the tail board. Use ½-inch pins with a slope of 1:6. The tails are 1½ inches wide.

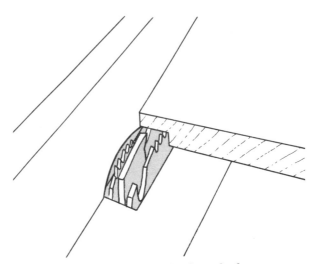

Illus. 12-8. After you have glued up the bottom panel, cut a barefaced tongue on all four edges. Set the dado blade to make a cut wider than ⅜ inch. Attach an auxiliary wood fence to the saw fence. With the saw lowered below the table, adjust the fence so that ⅜ inch of the blade is exposed. Then turn on the saw and raise the blade to ⅜ inch. The saw is now set up to cut the tongue. Place the bottom (Part C) with its outside face against the saw table. Cut a tongue on all four edges. Refer to Chapter 6 for directions on making tongue-and-groove joints.

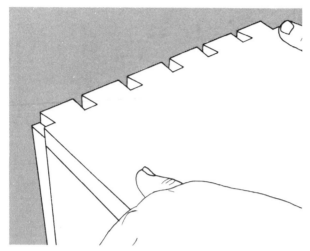

Illus. 12-9. At this point, assemble the box. Apply glue to the first dovetail joint and put it together, as shown here. Next, place the tongue of the bottom (Part C) in the grooves. Don't use any glue on this joint. When the bottom is in place, assemble the rest of the dovetail joints.

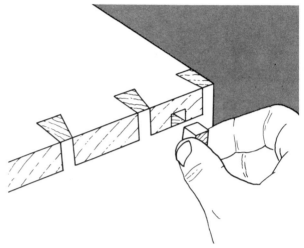

Illus. 12-10. The end of the groove shows on the last tail. Cut a small piece of wood to fit into the groove, and glue it in place. Apply glue only to the edges of the block; don't use too much glue. If glue runs into the groove, it could glue the bottom in place and cause it to split later.

this joint. The bottom "floats" in the grooves. The reason for leaving the bottom loose in the groove is to allow the bottom to shrink or swell as the air humidity changes. If you glue the bottom in place, it will eventually split or push apart one of the corner joints.

Once the bottom is in place, assemble the rest of the dovetail joints. When the box is assembled, you will notice that the end of the groove shows. There are variations on the dovetail joint that would cover this, but in this project just cut a small piece of wood and glue it into the end of the notch to fill it. (See Illus. 12-10.) If you are interested in using a joint that will account for the end of the groove, consult *Wood Joiner's Handbook.*

Now, cut out the handles. The bottom edge of the handle is bevelled to give you a better grip. Set the blade tilt to 25 degrees and rip a strip of wood long enough to make both handles. The ends of the handles are also bevelled. Make the cut in the same way you would make a case mitre. Set the blade tilt to 45 degrees. Use the mitre gauge to guide the board. (See Illus. 12-11.)

A pegged joint is used to attach the handles. Apply glue to the back of the handles; then clamp

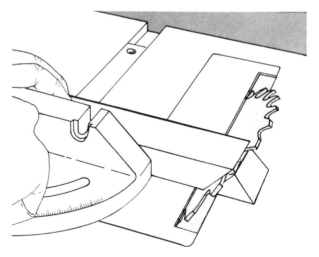

Illus. 12-11. The bottom edge of the handle is bevelled to give you a better grip. Set the blade tilt to 25 degrees and rip a strip of wood long enough to make both handles. The ends of the handles are also bevelled. Make the cut in the same way you would make a case mitre. Set the blade tilt to 45 degrees and use the mitre gauge to guide the board, as shown here.

them in place on the ends of the box. Drill two 5⁄16-inch-diameter holes through the handle and all the way through the end (Part B). Apply glue to the inside of the holes. Drive 1¾-inch-long dowels into the holes. The dowels are slightly long, so trim them flush after the glue dries. They can be cut from a length of standard dowel stock.

For a more authentic-looking joint, start with a square piece of oak 5⁄16 × 5⁄16 × 1¾ inches. Use a chisel to bevel off the corners so that you have an octagonal peg. (See Illus. 12-12.)

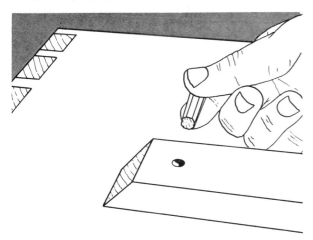

Illus. 12-12. A pegged joint is used to attach the handles. Apply glue to the back of the handles, and then clamp them in place on the box. Drill two 5⁄16-inch-diameter holes. The holes are located ⅞ inch up from the bottom of the handle and 1¾ inches in from the ends of the handle. The dowels can be cut from a length of standard dowel stock. For a more authentic-looking joint, use an octagonal peg.

Now make the lid. The lid is a framed panel. The same construction techniques can be used to make panel doors. Rip enough stock to width to make the stiles (Part E) and the rails (Part F). Next, set up the table saw to cut a ¼-inch-wide × ⅜-inch-deep groove. Adjust the fence to center the groove on the edge of the board. Cut a groove on the inside edge of all of the stiles and rails. (See Illus. 12-13.)

Now, cut the stiles and rails to length. Add 1½ inches to the length shown in the Bill of Materials for the stiles (Part F) to add a horn, if you will be chopping the mortises by hand. The length for the rails (Part F) given in the Bill of Materials includes the length of through tenons.

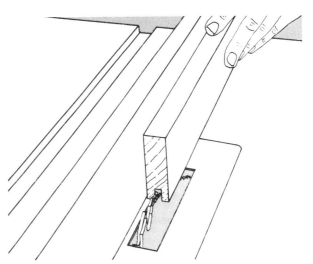

Illus. 12-13. To make the lid, first rip enough stock to width to make the stiles (Part E) and the tails (Part F). Then set up the table saw to cut a ¼-inch-wide × ⅜-inch-deep groove. Adjust the fence to center the groove on the edge of the board. Cut a groove on the inside edge of all of the stiles and rails.

Lay out the mortise-and-tenon joints. (See Chapter 9.) The plans show a through, haunched mortise and tenon, but an open mortise-and-tenon joint can be used. Chop the mortise using one of the methods shown in Chapter 9. (See Illus. 12-14.) The mortising chisel works well in this situation, since the groove will help guide the chisel as you start the cut.

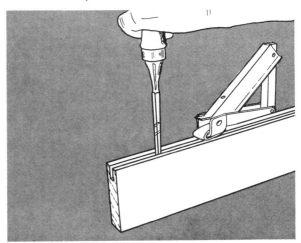

Illus. 12-14. Chop the mortise using one of the methods shown in Chapter 9. The mortising chisel works well in this situation, since the groove will help guide the chisel as you start the cut.

Cut the tenons on the ends of the rails. The haunched tenon is used to fill in the end of the groove that is exposed on the end of the stiles. (See Illus. 12-15.)

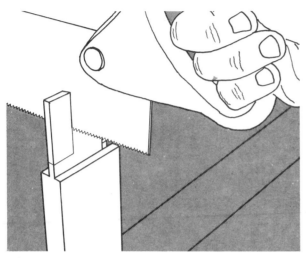

Illus. 12-15. Cut the tenons on the ends of the rails. A haunched tenon is used, because it will fill in the end of the groove that is exposed on the end of the stiles. You can use any of the methods described in Chapter 9 to make the tenons. Either lay out and cut the haunch at the same time you cut the rest of the tenon, or cut a standard tenon and then lay out the haunch and cut it with a backsaw.

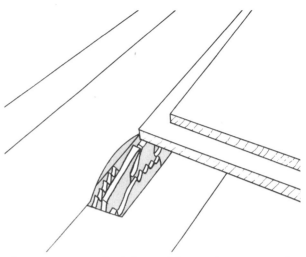

Illus. 12-16. Cut the lid panel (Part G) to size, and then cut a ⅜-inch tongue on all four edges. Set up the table saw to cut the tongue. Since the panel is large, place its face against the saw table and its edge against the fence. When assembling the lid, apply glue to the mortise-and-tenon joints, but don't use any glue in the tongue-and-groove joint for the panel. The panel "floats" in the frame. Leaving the panel loose allows for dimensional change due to variations in moisture content.

Now, cut the lid panel (Part G) to size. The size listed in the Bill of Materials includes a ⅜-inch-tongue on all four edges. Set up the table saw to cut the tongue. Since the panel is large, place its face against the saw table and its edge against the fence. (See Illus. 12-16 and Chapter 6.)

Assemble the lid. Apply glue to the first mortise and tenon and assemble the joint; then insert the panel. Don't use any glue in the tongue-and-groove joint for the panel. The panel "floats" in the frame. Leaving the panel loose allows for dimensional change due to variations in moisture content.

Now, assemble the rest of the mortise-and-tenon joints. Clamp the joints until the glue sets.

All that is left to do is to install the hardware and finish the box. T-shaped strap hinges were used to install the lid for the joiner's box shown in this chapter, but another type can be used. This box is a good size for a toy box, but if you plan on using it around small children, be sure to use special toy-box hardware. Toy-box hardware has a lid support that will keep the lid from hitting a child on the head.

If you are adept at carving, you can decorate the box with a name or date or other design. I chose to make the box look like it was over a hundred years old, so I simulated the wear the box would have received in that amount of time. If you want to do the same, use a belt sander to round all of the corners and edges. Make some nicks and dents in the box by hitting it with things such as keys, punches, and chains. Finish the box as you choose. A medium oak Danish-oil finish gives the box an authentic look.

GLOSSARY

Barefaced Joint A joint in which one or more of its shoulders are eliminated. (See Shoulder.)

Baseboard A moulding covering the joint of a wall and the adjoining floor. (See Moulding.)

Bead A projecting moulding with a half-round profile.

Bevel An inclined, angled, or slanted edge; not at a 90-degree angle.

Blind Joint A joint cut only partially through the board so that the end grain is hidden.

Box Joint A joint with multiple interlocking fingers, usually used to make boxes.

Butt Joint A joint in which the edge or end of one board is butted against another.

Carcass The basic box of a cabinet; the basic frame.

Case Joint A joint used to join the end of one board to the face of another. Case joints are used to make boxes, cabinets, and shelves.

Chuck An attachment for holding a workpiece or tool in a machine.

Dado Blade The blade used on a table saw to cut dado joints. The *stack dado blade* consists of a set of two blades and several chippers. The width of the dado is determined by the combination of chippers placed between the blades. The *wobbler dado blade* consists of a single blade that wobbles back and forth to create a cut that is wider than the blade.

Dado Joint A T-shaped case joint that is used to make boxes, cabinets, and shelves.

Dovetail Joint A case joint in which tapered pins fit into sockets between flared tails.

Dowel Joint A butt joint that is reinforced with wood pegs called dowels. Dowel joints are used in cabinets and bookcases, and to joint the parts of a chair or table legs to a rail.

Edges The narrower flat surfaces of a board that are parallel to the grain.

Edge Grain The term applied to the fibre orientation of the board edge.

Edge Joint A joint used to join the edge of one board to the face of another. Edge joints are often used when applying trim or face frames to a cabinet.

End Grain A term that refers to the porous ends of the fibres.

Face Grain The direction of the wood fibres on the face of the board.

Faces The two flat surfaces of a board that are wider than the other surfaces.

Flush Directly abutting or immediately adjacent.

Frame Joint A joint used to join the end of one board to the edge of another. They are used to make door frames and similar items.

Grain The orientation of the fibres in the wood, or a term used to describe the visible pattern of pores and growth rings on a board.

Hardboard A sheet material made from compressed wood fibres.

Kerf The area that is cut away by the saw blade.

Lap Joint A joint with a large amount of long-grain gluing surface that is used primarily on all kinds of frames.

Marking Gauge   Is used to lay out lines parallel to the edges of a board.

Mitre Gauge   The part of a table saw that slides in the mitre slot, which is cut into the table and runs parallel to the saw blade. The mitre gauge is used to control stock when it is being cut.

Mitre Joint   A highly decorative joint that is used for frame, case, and edge joints, and can be used to join boards at odd angles.

Mortise-and-Tenon Joint   A joint in which a projection called a tenon on one board fits into a pocket called a mortise in the other board.

Moulding   A wood surface shape, or a narrow strip that is used primarily for decoration.

Panel Joint   Joints used to join two or more narrow boards together into a larger panel.

Particleboard   A sheet material made from pressed wood chips or wood particles.

Plywood   A sheet material made by gluing together thin layers of wood.

Rabbet Joint   A corner joint with one shoulder that is one of the most common joints used in cabinetmaking. A rabbet joint is often used to join the top of a cabinet to its sides, and to attach the back of a cabinet.

Rails   The horizontal sides to a frame.

Rip Fence   An accessory on the table saw that is used to control stock when you are ripping (cutting with the grain).

Shoulder   The part of the joint that is cut 90 degrees to the face or edge of the board. A joint only has a shoulder when that part of the board that fits into a joint must be thinner or narrower than the rest of the board.

Siding   Boards that form the exposed surface of outside walls of frame buildings.

Spline Joint   A joint that is reinforced by a thin piece of wood called a spline. The spline fits into a groove that is cut into both mating surfaces of the joint.

Sliding T Bevel   A layout tool designed to lay out a bevel, a mitre, or an angle.

Square   To ensure that all corners of a workpiece form perfect right (90-degree) angles.

Stiles   The vertical sides of a frame.

Stop Block   A true piece of stock that is clamped to the table, fence, or mitre gauge of a table saw or radial arm saw. A stop block is shopmade; it locates one end of the part to be cut. This end should already be square. The distance from that end to the blade is the desired length of the part.

Tenon Jig   An accessory used on a table saw to help cut tenons. It fits into the mitre gauge slot, and has clamps that hold the work as the cut is made.

Tongue-and-Groove Joint   A two-part joint in which a projection on one board called a tongue fits into a groove in the other board.

Through Joint   A joint that is cut all the way through one board so that the end grain of the other board shows on the face of the first one.

Metric Equivalents

INCHES TO MILLIMETRES AND CENTIMETRES

MM—millimetres   *CM—centimetres*

Inches	MM	CM	Inches	CM	Inches	CM
⅛	3	0.3	9	22.9	30	76.2
¼	6	0.6	10	25.4	31	78.7
⅜	10	1.0	11	27.9	32	81.3
½	13	1.3	12	30.5	33	83.8
⅝	16	1.6	13	33.0	34	86.4
¾	19	1.9	14	35.6	35	88.9
⅞	22	2.2	15	38.1	36	91.4
1	25	2.5	16	40.6	37	94.0
1¼	32	3.2	17	43.2	38	96.5
1½	38	3.8	18	45.7	39	99.1
1¾	44	4.4	19	48.3	40	101.6
2	51	5.1	20	50.8	41	104.1
2½	64	6.4	21	53.3	42	106.7
2	76	7.6	22	55.9	43	109.2
3½	89	8.9	23	58.4	44	111.8
4	102	10.2	24	61.0	45	114.3
4½	114	11.4	25	63.5	46	116.8
5	127	12.7	26	66.0	47	119.4
6	152	15.2	27	68.6	48	121.9
7	178	17.8	28	71.1	49	124.5
8	203	20.3	29	73.7	50	127.0

Index